Those Sisters Can Preach!

Those Sisters Can
PREACH!

22 Pearls of Wisdom, Virtue and Hope

Edited by
Vashti Murphy McKenzie

THE
PILGRIM
PRESS
Cleveland

The Pilgrim Press
700 Prospect Avenue
Cleveland, Ohio 44115
thepilgrimpress.com

17   16   15   14   13   5   4   3   2   1

A catalogue record for this book is available from the Library of Congress
ISBN 978-0-8298-1984-7

CONTENTS

INTRODUCTION

Preaching is the divine encounter between God, the preacher, and those who would hear God's proclaimed Word. In order for authentic preaching to occur, the preacher must have a transforming relationship with God, about whom she or he speaks. Preaching must be viewed as a spiritual discipline that is approached with a determination to bring forth excellence in biblical scholarship, oratorical effectiveness, and a profound connectedness to the ones to whom the preacher brings the Word of God.

In the African American context, preaching has been considered as both a folk and a fine art; hence, it cannot simply be viewed as communication alone. For in the African American pulpit, there are unique expectations of the black preacher, which are different from those in other cultural contexts. The black preacher must bring the totality of herself or himself to the message, yet the message cannot become about the preacher, for then it will veer from the biblical mandate to preach the gospel. The message must be biblically based and rooted in the preacher's relationship with God and the preacher's connection to the Holy Spirit. The message must both encourage us and call us to accountability.

There is no room in the contemporary African American pulpit for vacuous preaching, preaching that neither effectively proclaims the message of the gospel nor significantly engages the hearer. Rather, today, in an age when 80 percent of Americans in the millennial generation have never been inside a church, there continues to be a need for a proclaimed word that reaches to the hearts of the unreached masses.

Those Sisters Can Preach! 22 Pearls of Wisdom, Virtue and Hope brings together twenty-two of the most powerful African American female preachers in this nation. Each one brings her unique and extraordinary perspective to the proclamation of the Word of God. There are messages of Old Testament power and New Testament hope. There are messages that call the body of Christ to accountability and messages that speak directly to the issues of Christian women in what seems almost like a personal conversation.

Those Sisters Can Preach! is a marvelous example of the kind of preaching that is needed in the church today. These mighty women of God, who stand on the shoulders of Sojourner Truth and Jarena Lee, are examples of the many extraordinary women who bring the truth of God's Word to the people of God each week. They are the trailblazers who will set in stone the foundation for a new generation of female preachers who will come behind them, who will not experience the obstacles to their calling and ministry that these twenty-two trendsetters have endured.

As you experience each of these powerful sermons, you will find yourself in each of these messages of hope, courage, and renewal. These women of God stand in the gap, Sunday after Sunday, sharing a message of hope and liberty that was often denied to them . . . even within the context of the church. Nonetheless, they are able to bring an extraordinary message of God's power and ability to their hearers, who are sorely in need of this proclamation.

You are invited to journey into the heart of each of these preachers as they bring forth their messages of transformation and rebirth, and as they deliver the gospel through their own unique lens. You are invited to embrace these messages, which come from preachers who are considered some of the greatest and most well-known preachers in the land, and messages that come from the hearts of some new prophetic voices on the horizon. *Those Sisters Can Preach! 22 Pearls of Wisdom, Virtue and Hope* is a collection of sermons that will lift your spirit, touch your heart, and elevate your mind. Allow these messages of faith and challenge to inspire you to greater heights in faithfulness, and to a deeper level of connectedness to God.

CHAPTER 1

IT'S A SET-UP

Vashti Murphy McKenzie

Read: Ruth 2:1–14

Lewis Carroll's classic children's story *Alice's Adventures in Wonderland* has seen many reincarnations from silent movies, a television series, a made-for-TV movie, cartoon adaptations, all the way to Tim Burton's recent sequel. The story plays with logic in such a way that it is has become a perennial favorite of children and adults.

Alice comes to a fork in the road and asks the wily Cheshire cat a direction and destination question. Which direction should I take? The cat responds, "That depends a good deal on where you want to go." "I don't much care where," says Alice. "Then," says the cat, "it doesn't matter which way you walk."

Life is filled with swift transitions but it is also filled with decisions. Some decisions do not reach our conscious mind, like which shoe to put on first or which way to drive home. These decisions are made out of habit.

There are decisions that require a bit more thought and time. Which power suit to wear? Which e-mails do I answer or ignore? Do I tweet or text? Should I use Facebook or MySpace? Which movie should I watch on my phone? Should I eat in or eat out? These appear to be insignificant and small decisions, but woven together they represent the tapestry of everyday life.

Then there is the hard stuff. The life-altering decisions: Do you keep looking for the job you want or take the job you're offered? Do you start your business in an uncertain economy? Do you run for office against an incumbent? Do you take a shortcut to success that may be

1

short-lived? Should you do it—whatever it is—because everyone else is doing it? Do you put him out or let him spend the night? Am I willing to accept the invitation to be the other woman? If I tell the lie, can I get away with it? Should I put in a transfer? Pursue another line of business? This is hard stuff to decide—destination and direction questions that deserve a great deal of thought.

You could always rely on your gut, but do you really want to base all your decisions upon your feelings? You could stick with gathering and analyzing data, but do you want to leave your heart out? Besides, if you dwell too long on facts and figures, it could lead to the "paralysis of analysis."

There are those who fear making the hardest decisions because they are afraid the right decision may require more hard work. It may challenge you beyond your capabilities. It may end your "trying to please everyone all the time" thing. It may cause haters to be upset because you have stepped onto the playing field and changed the way the game is played—when the haters were happy when you merely watched the game. It may also cause rejection by those who disagree with you or may decrease available resources. It may test your patience, stir up your gifts, or force those closest to you to treat you differently because you are doing something differently. The right decision may result in loneliness, involve you hurting someone's feelings, or actually lead to your destiny. It's hard sometimes to make the right decision.

It is possible to be swayed to make the wrong decision. Ask Eve in the garden or Haman at the gate of the city, or the rich young ruler.

Ori Brafman in the bestselling book *Sway: The Irresistible Pull of Irrational Behavior* writes about how people are swayed to make the wrong decision. All of us want to make the best decision using a sound thought process that includes reason and concrete data. But that doesn't always happen. Brafman indicates that when we feel particularly stressed or there's a lot on the line we become vulnerable to psychological forces that make us more likely to make choices not in our best interest. We will do anything to avoid a loss, even if it is not in our best interest. We move quickly to avoid a loss but not as fast to obtain a gain. We don't realize we're being swayed.

We cash in an investment because we are afraid of losing money. We change jobs because we're afraid we might be fired. We hold on too tightly in a relationship because we're afraid we're going to lose the person. Brafman calls it "loss aversion," people's tendency to feel the pain associated with a loss twice as intensely as the joy ascribed to an equivalent-sized gain.

Decisions—whether they are right or wrong, good or bad, wise or poor—decisions are a part of our everyday lives. Yes, there are two sides to every decision just as there are two sides to fly paper—and it makes a big difference to the fly which side it chooses.

Steven Covey writes in his book *First Things First: Coping with the Ever-Increasing Demands of the Workplace* that every day of our lives, in that split second between inspiration and execution, there are hard moments, hard moments where decisions are made that impact and determine our future.

Our text gives us a glimpse of a group of people up to their noses in making decisions—decisions that had an impact upon a family for generations to come and puts one of them in the lineage of the coming Messiah, Jesus.

Sandwiched between the era of the judges and era of the kings is the book of Ruth. On the surface, it appears to be a wonderful story of a second chance at love. Dig a little deeper and you'll find a story of how to start over after the decisions you've made. The book of Ruth flows more like a novella in four chapters than a book of historical data. The author excellently weaves the details as a tapestry of threads colored by struggle and a crisis of faith bought on by prolonged suffering.

The author speaks as one who is sitting close to the events—one who is more like a sympathetic pastor than a detached theologian or philosopher who intended the book to be a contribution in an ongoing high-level discussion of major theological pontifications.

The story begins simply with a destination and direction decision. There is a famine in the land. A great recession has gripped the little town of Bethlehem and its community. The city can't provide the resources to sustain its residents.

What had been a good life has now turned tedious and tasteless. The soil couldn't yield a harvest; herds and other animals were in danger of perishing for the lack of nourishment. Unemployment rates were up and assets were a diminishing reality. Elimelech, the head of the household, faced a tough decision. Does he keep the house in the suburbs or relocate his family to where the cost of living index is not so high? Can he afford to ride out the volatile economic forecast or should he cut his loses? Tough decisions.

If Elimelech stays in Bethlehem, he may put his family at risk of starvation. If he goes, there is no job guarantee in a country that is not his own. Direction and destination issues. Should he stick with what he knows or move his family outside the circle of family, friends, and faith?

Loss potential can push you to make decisions you wouldn't ordinarily make. Pain avoidance decisions could turn out to be the ones you later look back on and ask: Why did I make that decision?

Elimelech moved the family to Moab. The book is silent about the decision process. Did he pray about it? Consult others? Was this a God-led decision? The family settled in their adopted country. His two sons matured and they took wives from their new culture.

Trials came rushing in like floodwaters from a broken dam. First, the husband Elimelech dies, and then the two sons, leaving Naomi and her two daughter-in-laws, Ruth and Orpah, to fend for themselves. Grief gripped Naomi's heart and tears dripped down her cheeks. Misery came company-calling and depression cast a midnight shadow until this woman, whose name meant "pleasant," began to call herself Mara, meaning "bitter."

Hmmm. Elimelech's name meant "my god and my king." Their sons' names had special meaning. Mahlon's name meant "sickness" and Chilion's name meant "used up." For God's sake, be careful what you name your children. They just might live up to their names! Elimelech's name meant "my god and my king," but God was silent. Remember, when we feel particularly stressed or there's a lot on the line, we can become vulnerable to psychological forces that can sway our decision-making capability.

You can imagine how the three women felt. They are bereaved by the loss of their husbands. Naomi is separated from her family and community; she is in a strange place and a strange season in her life.

Naomi tells her daughters-in-law to return to their fathers' houses. There's nothing she can do to help them, and she will return to Bethlehem. Orpah leaves, but Ruth cleaves to Naomi. She refuses to leave Naomi. They share the good times and the not-so-good times together.

Ruth declares, "Your family is my family; your God is my God." Yet God is silent. When God seems silent about our situations, it seems

God does not care. The God's silence was one of the great issues of Calvary. When Jesus bore our sins and carried our sorrow, suddenly the sun began to hide its face, and the shadows of darkness blackened the sky. There were only the shrieks, curses, and tears of the people at the foot of the cross. There was only the anguished cry—my God, my God, why?

When it seems God has nothing to say, be sure that your imagination doesn't stray beyond the promises of God. It may look like nothing is going on. It may appear that God is absent, but God is "working behind the scenes rearranging the props," writes Ralph West. God is getting ready for the next act.

Ruth was penniless and worried about the future. She was in survival mode. Have you ever been there? She was making the best of a bad deal.

They are coming out of an economic holocaust arriving back in Bethlehem just in time for the barely harvest. Then, suddenly, Ruth had more than she needed dropped into her lap. Ruth hadn't earned it nor deserved it and couldn't understand it, but that's how God works.

Survival meant gleaning the fields. By law, the fringes of the field were left to the poor, penniless, widows, and orphans after the reapers had harvested the grain. It's as if Ruth felt this was all she could do.

The reapers began to deliberately drop handfuls of barley in her path. She started picking up underserved blessings because Boaz saw Ruth and told his workers to leave them for her.

Even Boaz had never spoken to Ruth, and still she received the blessing. Here's a thought. You never know what God has spoken over your life, but suddenly things change. Doors open. Opportunities come. People you thought hadn't noticed you or even liked you start to show you favor. God can put you in situations where others do the work and you get the benefit.

This story reminds us as long as there is life, there is always the possibility of sudden reversal. We still believe in the all-efficiency and the omnipotence of God. Do we still believe—God rewards those who earnestly seek him (Heb. 11:6)?! Do we still believe—God has plans for us, plans not to harm but to prosper us to give us a future and a hope (Jer. 29:11)?! Do we still believe—nothing is impossible to God (Luke 1:37)?! Do we still believe—God desires that we prosper and be in good health, just as our soul prospers (3 John 2)?! Do we still believe—that he who began a good work in you will complete it until the day of Christ Jesus (Phil. 1:6)?! Do we still believe—God will renew my strength (Isa. 40:31)?! Do we still believe—God is the one who will give us success (Nehemiah 2:20)?! Do we still believe—we are more than conquerors (Rom. 8:37)?! Do we still believe—we should purify ourselves from everything that contaminates the body and spirit?! (2 Cor. 7:1)?! Do we still believe—God is able to do far more abundantly beyond all that we ask?! (Eph. 3:20)?! Do we still believe—now these three remain: faith, hope and love, but the greatest of these is love (1 Cor. 13:13)?!

If so, then you must believe it is God who turns things around. We are in desperate need of sudden turnarounds. Things for which we advocated are forgotten in the minutia of the day. Family life is being sacrificed upon the altar of need and greed. More students are dropping out of school than those dropping in. Leadership is enjoying public success and private failure or public success and public failure. Commentary is confused with objective news reporting. People are living in toxic relationships. The bills continue to come in the mail and we continue to make them. Children keep borrowing. Friends keep betraying. Plans keep failing. Stuff keeps happening. Challenges keep coming and enemies keep scheming. If ever we needed a sudden turnaround, it is now.

Turnaround, a sudden divine turnaround like the kind Moses found at the edge of the Red Sea. The kind that Joshua found when the Jericho walls came tumbling down. The kind of turnaround the three Hebrew boys experienced suddenly in a fiery furnace. The turnaround Jeremiah experienced when he was suddenly pulled out of the pit, or the bent-over woman who went to church bent and went home standing straight and upright, or the man by the pool of Bethesda. The lepers, who lived with a deadly prognosis, were told to go show themselves to the priest. Someone needs encouragement—not to give up or walk away but to pray with me that God will move in a mighty way. God can turn it around.

Ruth said to Boaz, "Why do you favor me? You don't even know me." Can I make a suggestion? It was a set-up! Is it possible that the decisions that led to misfortune and miscalculation were used to set up the next level of blessings? Here we have two women who help each other in hard times. They are more like sisters than in-laws;

the older advising the younger; Naomi mentoring Ruth by taking her under her wings, and Ruth doing what only she could do, work the fields so they had food to eat.

Ruth's blessings—the subsequent purchase of Elimelech's land and Ruth's marriage to Boaz—benefited Naomi. One woman's blessing also blessed the other woman, so instead of trying to block your sister's blessing, help your sister get blessed. Second-hand blessings may come your way—residual blessings. Naomi's elevation may be your upgrade. Her climb may lift you up a little bit higher. It was a set-up!

Ruth had to work the fields before her blessing showed up. There are times God changes situations for us, but because we do not understand we have some part to play, an obligation or responsibility, we find ourselves in the same old situations. God can give us a new job, but we must have a new work ethic to keep it. God gives us the desires of our hearts to start something, but it will take discipline to finish something. God can turn our financial situation around, but if we refuse to tithe or refuse to budget, we will be broke real soon.

Everyone needs a new beginning. We all needs to know we can start over again, even in our winter years. But it means moving on to something new.

"Get up," God says. It's time to leave some old stuff behind, some old sickness, sick relationships, grief, or tears, and embrace a new wholeness. Leave the restrictive lifestyle of sin, ascend from the depths of despair and depression. Get up. Decide today you will not live in abuse. You will not settle for less. If what you're doing is too draining, debilitating, or just crazy, remember, God can turn it around.

The hand of God was working behind the scenes of Naomi and Ruth. God spoke favor over one woman's life and the other woman received the benefits—benefits she didn't have to work for. It was a set-up!

There are three points I want to share in this sermon. First, you need a sister to lean on in time of need. Second, my blessing is her blessing and her blessing is my blessing. Third, you are never too tired to start over again because everybody needs a new beginning. It's a set-up because nothing is impossible with God.

No matter how deep the water or the depth of the muck and mire of international politics, we are reminded that nothing is impossible with God. No matter how tense the environment or how crazy the situation, there is nothing impossible with God. No matter how iffy the chapter or strained the relationship between sisters, there is nothing impossible with God. No matter the state of the economy, the volatile ups and downs of the stock market, no matter the confusion or chaos, there is nothing impossible with God. It matters not how much our hearts are filled with fear, distress, or stress, we can be clear that no problems are too complex, no wounds too deep, no fracture unmendable, no physical challenge too far gone or issues too strange for God to handle.

God used a tough decision to put Ruth into position to be used in the plan of redemption. It was a set-up!

CHAPTER 2

UNSHAKABLE

Carla J. Debnam

Read: Hebrews 12:25–29 NLT

There are times in life when it seems like all hell is breaking lose. Can I get a witness? Maybe it was the death of a loved one, an unexpected illness, a home foreclosure, or a job loss that preceded your descent into darkness. Sometimes it is not an external event but an internal struggle that precipitates the confusion and chaos in your life. Regrets from poor decisions haunt you. Your mind won't let you forget your flaws. Those around you remind you of your shortcomings instead of your possibilities. Or you feel your potential has been snuffed out by your past. All of these can lead you to feel helpless and hopeless. Whatever the source of the problem, maybe we are encouraged by the witness of those who have endured the struggle before us and who have showed us how to lean on our faith.

In the text, we read the conclusion of the great passage of scripture encouraging the saints to continue fighting the good fight of faith. They are reminded that by focusing on Jesus and enduring God's discipline through divine correction and love we are shaped and molded in God's image. The book of Hebrews addresses the struggle the saints of that time would have faced, and it encouraged them in the face of persecution and hopelessness to live a life of faith. The writer uses this opportunity to remind them, and us today, that the battle is not over. Many have gone through tough times before us and survived, and so will we. There is hope in the midst of hell because we serve the God of the unshakable kingdom. The question we must answer is "What makes me *unshakable* in times like these?" Here are three important points about this passage.

First, *learn to listen.* You and I can be survivors and unshakable when we listen to and follow the directions of God. Verse 25 makes it plain. "*See to it that you obey God, the one who is speaking to you. For if the people of Israel did not escape when they refused to listen to Moses, the earthly messenger, how terrible our danger if we reject the One who speaks to us from heaven!*" The scripture makes it clear that, when Moses spoke, those who did not obey suffered the consequences of their disobedience. Likewise, so will those who hear the words of God and choose to ignore them. We often hear the cliché, "We have two ears so we can listen more than we speak." This is true especially when the we are listening to is God. God speaks to us through our circumstances, our community, God's word, the Holy Spirit, and our experiences. I believe God makes God's will clear. We often turn a deaf ear because it is not the word we want to hear, or we choose to receive a partial word but not the entire message. We love to quote, "God gives us the desires of our heart" without fully reading the text, which begins by telling us to "take delight in the Lord."

We have taken parts of the Word of God and combined them with other means of communication and gotten God's word twisted. We can't be doers of the word because we haven't first become hearers of the word. God wants you and I to begin listening and responding in faith so that we can get the full blessings and promises God has declared are ours. We are like some of our children who have developed selective hearing. They cannot hear when we call them to complete chores but they can hear us plain and clear when we offer to buy them the latest Jordans. God's commands are for our good, and we can become unshakable and unbreakable when we learn to listen and obey.

Second, *you are still standing.* Listening and obedience help us to abide in the Lord. The fact, however, that we are "still standing" is a sign of our fortitude and evidence that we are unshakable. "*When God spoke from Mount Sinai his voice shook the earth, but now he makes another promise: 'Once again I will shake not only the earth but the heavens also.' This means that the things on earth will be shaken, so that only eternal things will be left.*" God is serious about getting his people on the right track. He uses natural and supernatural signs and wonders to expose the true saints. Jesus said to the disciples, "You will know them by their fruit." Just like in health matters, you are what you eat. In spiritual matters you are what you produce. A healthy tree produces good fruit, whereas an unhealthy tree produces bad fruit.

God is shaking our foundations as individuals, families, churches, and countries. He wants to see who is left standing after the dust settles. Will you survive the shaking or be destroyed? The good news is those who have been washed in the blood of Jesus will remain standing. Jesus redeemed us from the path that lead to unrighteousness and put us in the path of everlasting life. We are still standing firm on the foundation of our faith in Jesus Christ. When the shaking comes to your life, be assured you will survive and remain unshakable.

Third, *respond in praise.* We can remain unshakable when we learn to listen, stand on the blood of Jesus Christ, and, finally, we remain victorious and unshakable when we respond to God's grace with praise. *"Since we are receiving a kingdom that cannot be destroyed, let us be thankful and please God by worshiping him with holy fear and awe."* The appropriate response to the grace and mercy we have received is to worship and praise God in spirit and in truth. We are heirs and joint heirs with Christ in an unshakable kingdom—a kingdom where we will lift up praises to God 24/7. Why should we wait to give God the honor God is due? We need to give God praise for looking beyond our faults and seeing our needs. A thankful heart seeks to please God and exhibits an enduring posture of faith and appreciation. Those who have been through a lot seem to get this. They know in their hearts how far the Lord has brought them.

Jesus described the woman with the alabaster jar in this way: "her sins which are many have been forgiven, so she has shown me much love. But a person who is forgiven little shows only a little love." I don't know about you, but my thanksgiving of God is as deep as the pit God found me in. We worship God in "holy fear" when we respect and revere God for who God is. God is good and God alone. There is no one like God and there never will be, we also should worship God in God's awesome glory. God surpasses anyone or anything we could ever imagine. Standing in awe of God means we fall down, bow down, and look away because God's face, God's presence is overwhelming. We can be unshakable when we give God the praise and worship out of our innermost being. Not a superficial praise but a praise that is authentic and genuine, a praise from the heart.

In conclusion, as the beginning of Hebrews chapter 12 states, "We are surrounded by such a huge crowd of witnesses to the life of faith." This crowd includes not only the witnesses stated in chapter 11, but also many others including you and me who have endured much, overcome much, and lived to share our testimony. We can become and remain unshakable when we learn to listen to and obey God, stand firm, and cultivate a heart of thanksgiving. I know that some of us share this testimony and victory is ours:

"My hope is built on nothing less than Jesus' blood and righteousness. I dare not trust the sweetest frame, but wholly trust in Jesus' name. When darkness seems to hide his lovely face, I rest on his unchanging grace. In every high and stormy gale, my anchor holds within the veil. On Christ the solid rock I stand, all other ground is sinking sand; all other ground is sinking sand."

CHAPTER 3

WALK IN IT

Felicia Sophronia Barwell

Read: Exodus 33:12–17 NIV

Many African American women pioneers have blazed the trails so that women of all walks of life can obtain previously unattainable opportunities. They have endured the deserts of life. Great African American women continue to inspire us in the twenty-first century. Women from Phyllis Wheatley to Sojourner Truth, Sally Hemings to Harriet Tubman, Mary Church Terrell to Ida B. Wells, Madame C. J. Walker to Mary McLeod Bethune, Maggie Lena Walker to Coretta Scott King, Fannie Lou Hamer to Rosa Parks, Lena Horne to Pearl Bailey, Angela Davis to Alice Walker, Dorothy Dandridge to Oprah Winfrey, Althea Gibson to Florence Griffith Joyner, Venus Williams to Mae Jemison, Shirley Chisholm to Barbara Jordan, Pauli Murray to Vashti Murphy McKenzie, and Marcia L. Fudge to Michelle Obama. Women have inspired humanity to rise from being in slavery to holding doctorate degrees, to become everything from songstress to activist, banker to entrepreneur, educator to author, Pulitzer prize winner to astronaut, lawyer to doctor, and to go from the poor house to the White House. Let's shout from the mountaintop that African American women have travailed and continue to travail over the stony and bittersweet roads of life. As we reflect on the successes of these and other women, we also must acknowledge there is still much work to accomplish. Resting on our morals is not an option, especially when we still face political, vocational, social, educational, and economic disparities and injustices.

Imagine all that these women had to endure. The challenges, obstacles, setbacks, dangers, closed doors, rejections, and ridicule. "My soul looks back and wonders" just how they got over, how they made it through. I contend it was by the favor, mercy, and grace of God. I contend it was the grace of God upon their lives. I contend they walked in grace. Through it all, they walked in the grace of God. Walking in grace embodies many benefits for believers.

As we look into the lens of the text and the life of Moses, let's discover the benefits of *prayer, presence, and power* from walking in grace. We are familiar with the biblical accounts of Moses and his commission to lead the people of God, the Israelites, from Egypt to the Promised Land. Further, we are familiar with their sinful ways of worshiping idols and how God dealt with them. This, however, is not our focus. Instead, turn your attention on Moses' walk. Meditate on the grace that God granted Moses and his walk in grace. For God said to Moses, "I will also do this thing that you have spoken; for you have found grace in *my* sight, and I know you by name."

Limiting grace to one definition would be paramount to putting God in a box. In the scriptures, grace can range from beauty, to favor, to love, and to acts of kindness. Walking in grace is an active, interactive manifestation of God in our divine purpose. Divine purpose is defined in our daily walk with God, our walk with one another, our doing the will of God, and our acceptance of the free gift of salvation. Grace, in the context of our text, is God extending Godself to Moses in order to meet the needs of the Israelites, and in order that Moses could carry out the mission to deliver the chosen people of God. As we enter our text, what an awesome place to find Moses in prayer with God. We know from the biblical account of Moses' journey that this certainly would not be his last prayer. Moses walked in prayer. It is suggested by scholars that Moses was face to face—as if talking with a friend—to emphasize the intimacy of his relationship with God. Prayer is about having a conversation with God—repeatedly, habitually. It is about a relationship, personal commitment. We know that prayer is a direct line of communication with God. It is personal, powerful, and healing, and sometimes we have to just sit and listen.

Moses had to be intentional about praying. He actually had to go outside of the camp to meet with God in prayer. Unlike us; we can pray any time and any place. We have easy access to God. We can walk in prayer morning, noon, and night. It doesn't mean we have to lay prostrate before God, head bowed, on bended knees. I am certain that many a prayer has been uttered while driving, in a meeting, taking a test, in the doctor's office, and even in the courthouse. It's not about the physical location or position. It is about having a humble heart and being in the spirit of prayer.

By the same token, we should be intentional about our prayer life and intentional about the time we devote to the nurturing and maturity of our relationship with God. Pray. We should always be intentional about our prayer life. There are times, however, when we have to just throw our heads back and say "Father, I stretch my hand to thee for there is no other help I know. Dear God, hear my prayer. I look, O God, to the hills from where not a little, not some, not much, but all of my help comes." Your prayer can be as simplistic as, "Now I lay me down to sleep, I pray O Lord, my soul to keep" or "Hallowed be they name, thy Kingdom come . . . ."

Moses was intentional about what he needed for the purpose of God's extraordinary commissioning. He was also persistent in asking God for God's presence. Note that Moses reminded God of God's promises. Moses was not challenging God, but seeking assurance. He says in verse 13, "If you are pleased with me, teach me your ways, so I may know you and continue to find favor with you. Remember that this nation *is* your people." In other words, God, did I hear you correctly? Are you sure it's me you want? I need to be certain. I need to know your ways. How do you want me to lead your people? Has God placed a calling on your life that you are dancing with? Are you waiting for the right time? Well the time is now. First, if we walk in prayer, God will, and does, answer our prayers.

Second, let's look at God's response to Moses' request for God's presence. Have you ever been asleep and woke up praying? I don't mean you awakened and started praying. I am talking about you awakened in prayer. What an awesome manifestation of God's presence.

God responded, Look, don't worry, Moses, "My Presence will go *with you*, and I will give you rest." I can see God in my spiritual eye, nodding to assure Moses, saying, "Yes, Moses, my child, on my behalf, you will have to walk this journey with and for the Israelites, and for those to come. I remind you once again I will be with you. My presence will be with you." But Moses was persistent about the dire need of God's presence on this journey. Moses wanted assurance, *blessed* assurance. He was not only asking for himself but also for the Israelites. Moses was interceding on behalf of the Israelites because they were not only exiled from their land but also alienated from God because of their sinful ways. I didn't say sinful nature but sinful ways. Moses knew in order to even attempt to carry out this great commission, the presence of God was a must. Oh yes, Moses had the grace and favor of God, but Moses also knew it would not be easy. Moses would face challenges and adversities from within the camp as well as external attacks. You know how it is sometimes when people in your very own circle seem to go against the grain. They simply walk to a different beat.

Moses, however, was intentional and persistent about praying. He asked God for God's presence. His persistence was not a challenge but demonstrating his level of commitment, dependence, and trust in God. Just because we repeatedly pray to God for something, it doesn't mean we don't have hope or believe. Just think about it, how many times have you told someone or God that you love them? How many times have you said, "Thank you, Lord" or praised the Lord? Saying it more than once doesn't mean it's any less true, important, or meaningful. No! So, be intentional and persistent. In other words Moses was saying, God, if I could only have the manifestation of your divine, holy, and righteous presence along the way, I know, Lord, that everything is going to be alright. No matter what I face, no matter the financial crisis, no matter the political crisis, no matter if work is lacking, no matter the drama, no matter, no matter, no matter. Everything is going to work out, because you, God, you know my name. You, God, have called me, you know me, and I am going to walk in and according to your grace.

People of God, we have not come this way without calamities, scrapes, and wounds but by the grace of God, by faith. In our daily walk, even in the mist of our struggles, we must first seek the presence of God. If we would just lean on God. Walking in the presence of God brings about wisdom, knowledge, and solutions when we don't have the answers. The presence of God brings about peace, protection, and comfort in our darkest hour. I don't know about you, but I find it difficult to be in prayer and not be in the presence of God. Likewise,

I find it difficult to be in the presence of God and not be in a state of prayer.

God gives us *power*. Not only should we walk in prayer, but we should walk in the presence of God. As we walk in the God's grace in prayer and in God's presence, the power of God is manifested. We not only need God's power to carry out physical activity but we need God's power to perform miraculously, exceedingly, and abundantly above and beyond anything you can possibly imagine. Moses had this power. Power. Most of the time, he wasn't even aware of his power until it was needed. Sure he had the physical stamina, energy, strength, and courage all given by the grace of God. But I am talking about the divine power. You have heard the stories of Moses parting the Red Sea, turning his rod into a serpent, changing the river from water to blood, and changing salty water to palatable drinking water. Moses was able to execute miracles by the power of God. The *power* God granted to Moses was by the grace of God. Moses had the power to lead God's people to liberation, and freedom. God demonstrated his *power* over, and over, and over. God's people were able to survive the heat and dust of the desert, the sickness, the death, and the enemies by the power of God.

We need our physical and mental strength and well-being to function. Oh, but think about those times when you couldn't put one foot in front of the other, didn't know which way to turn, where your next meal would come from, or how a bill might get paid; but somehow, somehow, you mustered up enough food to feed a hungry soul, you were able to minister to someone less fortunate, you were able to lead someone to the throne of God, and you were able to lay hands and anoint yourself. It was all by the power of God. I still can't figure out how it all came about. It was by the grace and holy power of God. Like Moses, you might have executed the task but it was only by the power of God that you were able to do so. Apart from the grace of God, apart from the power of God, we can do *nothing*!

God's grace is a gift. We have done nothing to deserve it. Don't let God's gift of eternal grace go to waste. Don't let what Jesus has done for me and you be in vain. We have grace that goes beyond the favor of God. God's grace will take you and me to the Promised Land. We have the grace that came by way of a baby Jesus, who walked the earth, hung on the cross in prayer with God, was raised from the dead with all power, and is in the presence of God. As believers, we have the presence of the living God, the presence of the Holy Spirit that abides within, and the holy presence we can walk in. Walk in the presence of the living God within you, and walk in the power of the Holy Spirit. We can't just receive the gift, say thank you, and never use it—like some gifts we receive knowing good and well we are never going to use them. Don't unwrap it. Just tuck it away some place or re-gift it and pass it on to someone else.

Are you walking in grace? Are you walking in the benefits of grace? Are you walking in prayer, prayer that rises up and makes you throw your head back and say, I need thee, oh, I need thee; every hour I need thee? Oh, but by the grace of God. Are you walking in the presence of God? Are you walking in the power of God? Walk in grace so you can do the work God has called you by name to do. Amen. Amen. Amen.

CHAPTER 4

UNMASKING FAMILY SECRETS:
What Wounds Are You Hiding?

Sekinah Hamlin

Read: 2 Samuel 13

A Bennett College alumna tells of the story of how she started in the community empowerment movement after college. She could not help but have the "change-agent" bug in her spirit—actually she had the flu! She ran a local community action agency for a while but decided to teach. She had plans to join the Teaching Corps to teach in rough schools where some people would be scared to go. She soon recognized, however, that teaching may not have been the best profession in which she could use her gifts. Instead, she believed she would be better suited in a position that gave her the ability to change social systems and eliminate oppression for the least of these.

In 1973, she went to work for another community action agency. One year later at the age of twenty-three she was promoted to executive director, with over a hundred full-time employees, a multistate territory, and a quarter-of-a-million-dollar budget. Her vision of being a change agent was being realized and she was expanding her reach to serve those underrepresented and left behind.

Life was good until a conversation she had with one of her board members. He disclosed that he was in charge of the National Guard when they were ordered to fire several rounds into the dormitories at North Carolina A&T State University after a student protest involving Dudley High School students and A&T students. The shooting occurred in 1969 when she was a student at Bennett College. This shooting is the subject of the documentary *Walls that Bleed*. The horrific event is likened to the Orangeburg massacre of 1968, the

Kent State shootings of 1970, and University of California at Berkeley uprisings of the late 1960s. What began as a protest over the results of a high school student government election where administrators were not responsive escalated when some student protesters solicited the help from nearby college students. The protest resulted in the death of one college student. The safe haven of North Carolina A&T had become a war zone where buildings designed to keep students safe became littered with holes and stained with blood. This event went largely unnoticed outside of the medium-sized southern town where it occurred in the backdrop of the nonviolent civil rights movement.

What would she do after this board member had shared his role in this historic destructive event? How would she deal with this secret? Could she in good conscience still "report" to someone who was involved in such a horrific event? Was this his attempt at reconciliation or said mainly just to clear his conscience?

Our text is a story of a family, a royal family with a painful secret. A family . . . Close your eyes and listen to our/their/her story. A story of a family—two brothers, a sister, a cousin, and a father (or a brother, a cousin, stepbrother, stepsister, and a father)

Amnon is the eldest brother, child of King David. He is the rightful heir to the throne. He has an insidious lust, a nagging desire for his beautiful untouched half-sister/stepsister, Tamar. He's sick with desire for her.

From the beginning, Tamar is seen as a female surrounded by two males. Her existence is seen in relationship to her brothers. She is encapsulated in the beginning text by "David's son Absalom had a beautiful sister whose name was Tamar; and David's son Amnon fell in love with her." Her introduction is sandwiched between the two men, and their story is given to stress their relation to King David. Yet, later in the story, Tamar is still viewed as that object that is commandeered, robbed of its value (her virginity), and left to lay desolate/to rot.

It is actually the story of Absalom. Absalom, though not directly involved in the beginning of the story, is the first sibling to be mentioned by the narrator. Even the rape of Tamar becomes a quest for Absalom to seek vengeance for his sister. In scripture, the story becomes necessary because the actions of Absalom brought forth a series of political crises with a decisive effect on the future of the nation. The deaths of Amnon, the eldest son, and ultimately the death of Absalom, opened the way for Solomon, who was originally far down the line of succession, to become king. Tamar is once again not the subject but an object at play in the story of her brothers and the succession to the throne.

She is invisible. Tamar, who begged for her life and tried to offer an alternative in which she recognized herself as property, had no say so in her consumption by Amnon. Tamar was the object of lust and the object of shame. Tamar . . .

The full story of Tamar is not recorded in the Word of God. We are challenged to think about how she must have felt. We are challenged to feel Tamar's pain. We are challenged to really see her as she tries to wash the dirt and filth off her body caused by this violation. We are challenged to live in the place of loneliness and shame in which Tamar was forced to live forever. We, however, are challenged to bring her good news. We are challenged to be her. *Yet I submit to you, this is not that far-fetched of a challenge. It is not that difficult.*

We have been and are Tamar. It does not matter if we are male or female. We have experienced some beatings in life that have left such severe wounds in our bodies that we did not know how we were going to continue living.

There are secrets being kept in our families, and we will not "air our dirty laundry." I submit three things we can glean from this pericope to unmask our family secrets.

Tamar was sexually assaulted, not by a stranger, but by someone she knew. Tamar's violation took place not in a dark alley or desolate park, but in her brother's home. Tamar was exploited through one of her most vulnerable traits—her kindness and upbringing to care for her family.

Tamar said no, but her "no" was not respected. Tamar sought help but was told to keep quiet. The process for achieving justice and restitution was taken out of Tamar's hands entirely and carried out by her brother— it was men's business. Tamar's father did not mourn for her. Rather, he mourned for her perpetrator. The end of Tamar's story happens without her. Just as Tamar's viewpoint does not matter, the existence of a mother or the mother of the children is not an issue either.

When we view people as property, if that property becomes damaged, the only recourse we have for our tarnished possession is to ask for a refund, seek restitution, or throw it out. For Amnon, scripture says the remedy was throwing it out. Scripture says for Absalom, the damaged property was made right by killing the one who damaged it. For Tamar, scripture says . . . nothing. You see, Tamar is the "it." She is the property in question. As Absalom goes to seek restitution, or give the equivalent of the injury done, he kills Amnon as Amnon has killed his sister.

From the beginning, Tamar was viewed as an object, as property. She was one whose legitimacy was granted only in as much as she related to men. Yet, whatever hope for personhood she may have had was destroyed by Amnon's robbing her of the one asset she had, her virginity.

So what happens when someone tears or rips at a part of you that is representative of a divine gift? What happens when someone reaches down in you with an uninvited force? What happens when the tears and rips are not just about the physical but the spiritual—an involuntary touching of the special place that, while physical, is inextricably tied to the divine gift and cannot be separated from your soul?

And whoever is the wielder of such destruction cannot believe in such divine gifts or God.

The rape of Tamar was the rape of her tomorrow. The beautiful virgin encircled has become the raped sister isolated. Her plight is the reason for silence and hatred.

Tamar's story is hidden/submerged under the male drama of political intrigue and destiny.

The response to the crime is most telling. Absalom waits two years, and then persuades his father to let Amnon visit at Baal Hazor along with the king's other sons. It was a brothers' feast of much wine, good food, and I'm sure plenty of women. But while Amnon was drunk, Absalom ordered his servants to kill him. The murder woke the other brothers, who mounted their mules and fled.

The news came to King David, who immediately tore his clothes and fell on the ground overtaken with grief and mourning for his eldest son, Amnon—the one with whom he shared the rapist bond.

Absalom then flees the country for three years.

Tamar's story cries out from the submersion. See me, hear me, know me, deal with me. I am a person. I was created in God's image. I am Tamar.

I am not simply the new citizen who you do not have time to talk to because my English is not perfect.

I am not simply the one who was made to feel embarrassed to asked questions in class because I have a learning difference, thus I am always silently seated in the back.

I am not simply the one who does not fit society's image of attractiveness—the one who was once the most attractive and energetic person at the party but now whose body has been deteriorated by multiple sclerosis.

I am not simply the one you see with my same-gender partner of twenty years holding hands in the mall but you choose to look the other way.

I am not simply the woman of color who cleans up after you but your greeting usually is, "You forgot to get the trash in the bathroom."

I am not simply the parent who once sacrificed so you could have the things in life I did not have, but now due to my ailing health has inconvenienced your life such that you have placed me in a nursing home and only send checks monthly.

I am not simply the one who gives of my musical gifts freely on Sunday only to go unacknowledged when you see me and my partner of many years in the grocery store.

I am a person. I was created in the image of God. I am Tamar. See me, hear me, know me, and deal with me. God created us all for community.

At the beginning of his ministry, Jesus proclaims that the Spirit of the Lord is upon him, for he has been anointed to bring good news to the poor. Jesus was sent to proclaim release to the captives and recovery of sight to the blind, to let the oppressed go free, to proclaim the acceptable year of the Lord's favor (Luke 4:18–19).

Jesus, who gives us freedom, is our advocate, our liberator. He models for us the proverb that calls us to "judge righteously and plead the cause of the poor and needy" (Prov. 31:9). Jesus modeled this in his defense of the woman who had many husbands and the acknowledgment and healing of the hemorrhaging woman.

For Absalom, advocacy and liberation meant only avenging the wrong brought upon his sister—taking matters into his own hands without the involvement of Tamar. Yet, advocacy and liberation is not always about speaking for or acting for the "other." It is often about creating space for the "other" to be seen—for the "other's" feelings, hurts, desires, and personhood to be respected. It's about listening, learning, knowing. It's about the reality that the "other" is us.

CHAPTER 5

REMEMBER GOD'S PROMISES

Jo Ann Browning

Read: Genesis 22 NIV

As believers, God has called us to be faithful, focused, and fearless as we journey through life. The order of the words themselves is important. The words represent a growth process—you can't be one thing without the other. In order to live fearlessly, you must be focused. In order to live focused, so that you can eventually live fearlessly, you must be faithful. It's a process.

The Bible is full of examples of people who were faithful. For example, Abraham's story has always strengthened my faith. His faith was exceedingly great. He was willing to do anything and everything that God asked of him, no matter what the personal cost.

In Genesis 22, God tests Abraham by telling him to sacrifice his only son, Isaac. Can you imagine being asked to sacrifice your child? Yet Abraham fully trusted God and was prepared to do what was required of him. He did not complain; he did not question God; he did not argue. Abraham prepared the altar to do God's will and sacrifice his beloved son.

As he raised the knife in the air, an angel of God stepped in and stopped Abraham from sacrificing his son. The angel said, "Do not do anything to him. Now I know that you fear God, because you have not withheld from me your son, your only son" (Gen. 22:12). God stepped in at the nick of time, not a moment too late, nor a moment too soon. Has God ever stepped into a situation that was testing your faith and instantly turned things around for you?

Abraham noticed a ram caught in a thicket by its horns. He took the ram and offered it up for a burnt offering instead of his son. Abraham called the place "The Lord Will Provide." I encourage you to take a lesson from Abraham. When God makes a provision in your life, give God his due. How often have you ever thought something happened for you, just at the right moment, by coincidence? It was no coincidence—it was God. The ram was not in the bush by coincidence. God put it there to make a way for Abraham, and God has put a ram in the bush for you too.

Not only did God spare Abraham's son's life, and make provision for him, God blessed Abraham beyond measure for Abraham's obedience. "I swear by myself, declares the Lord, that because you have done this and have not withheld your son, your only son, I will surely bless you and make your descendants as numerous as the stars in the sky and as the sand on the seashore. Your descendants will take possession of the cities of their enemies, and through your offspring all nations on earth will be blessed, because you have obeyed me" (Gen. 22:16–18). When you are obedient, God will bless you beyond all that you could ever think or imagine.

Abraham did not develop his deep, abiding trust in God overnight. To truly understand how God moved in Abraham's life, I need to take you back to the beginning of his life, back before he received God's blessing.

In Genesis 12, God tells Abraham, then called Abram, to leave his family, his father's house, his comfortable familiar life, and go to a land that God would eventually show him. But God also makes him a promise. God promises Abram he will make a great nation through Abram. God also promises Abram he will bless those who bless Abram and curse those who curse Abram. God promises Abram that all the families of the earth, and that includes you and me, will be blessed. Abram was obedient, when God spoke; he obeyed and he departed. You can rest assured that when God makes a promise to you, God will keep it.

When Abram starts his journey from Horan, he is seventy-five years old. With him are his wife, Sarai; Lot, his brother's son; and all of his earthly possessions. (Just because God told you to go, don't assume that the journey will be easy.) The Bible says when they got to the land of Canaan, they found it occupied by the Canaanites. But God appeared again and made another promise to Abram, "To your descendants I will give you this land." Abram continued on his journey, stopping at a place where Bethel was on the west and Ai on the east, where he pitched a tent and built an altar. Abram and his family traveled on towards the Negev. They eventually arrived in Egypt because in the land they left was a famine.

Here's where things get interesting: Sarai was a beautiful woman, and Pharaoh was captivated by her beauty. Fearing for his life, Abram tells Sarai to tell Pharaoh that she is his sister, not his wife. Abram is blessed with "sheep and cattle, male and female donkeys, menservants and maidservants, and camels." Don't let a lie block your blessings—anything you gain by lying will not last.

God was not pleased and sent a plague upon Pharaoh and his household. When Pharaoh discovers that the plagues occurred because of Abram's lie, he banishes Abram, Sarai, and all who were with him, including the servants and all of the livestock Pharaoh had given Abram, from Egypt. Abram returns to the Negev and eventually settles in the land between Bethel and Ai where he had previously built an altar. He builds another altar and calls on God again.

Abram's lie continues to wreak havoc in his life even after he has been banished from Egypt. Strife emerges between Abram's and Lot's men because the land where they had temporarily settled could not support the massive amount of livestock. So Lot and Abram go their separate ways. Lot chooses the plains of Jordan and pitches his tent near Sodom while Abram chooses to dwell in the land of Canaan.

Here's what I love about God: Even after the lie, and after Lot left Abram, the Bible says, God continued to make promises to Abram, "Lift up your eyes from where you are and look north and south, east and west. All the land that you see I will give to you and your offspring forever. I will make your offspring like the dust of the earth, so that if anyone could count the dust, then your offspring could be counted. Go, walk through the length and breadth of the land, for I am giving it to you," (Gen. 13:14–17). When God makes an investment in you, no matter what you do to mess things up, God will reposition you for success.

Lot becomes entangled in a war between kings, and as a result he and all of his possessions are taken captive. Abram gathers an army of 318 men and rescues Lot and retrieves his possessions. When the king of Sodom offers to make Abram rich, this time Abram knows better, "I have raised my hand to the Lord, God Most High, Creator of heaven and earth, and have taken an oath that I will accept nothing belonging to you, not even a thread or the thong of a sandal, so that you will never be able to say, 'I made Abram rich'" (Gen. 14:22–23). Do you see the difference in Abram? Part of becoming a faithful, focused, and fearless child of God is learning from your past mistakes and making a commitment to God not to repeat the same mistakes over and over again.

In Genesis 15:1, God assures Abram's future success, telling him "Do not be afraid, Abram. I am your shield, your very great reward." Although I believe Abram was grateful for God's protection, he wanted something more from the God; Abram wanted an heir, who was born of his own loins. And here is where the ultimate blessing begins to unfold. God not only promises to give Abram an heir, but he tells Abram his descendants will outnumber the stars in the heavens.

But you know how the story goes. Sarai suggests to Abram that he impregnate her maidservant, Hagar. So, at eighty-six years old, Abram fathers Ishmael; but while Hagar is pregnant, Hagar begins to despise Sarai. I cannot stress this fact enough, when you decide to go against God's will, even though your intentions may be right, your plan will never work if it goes against God's will for your life.

When Abram is ninety-nine years old, God appears to him again, and despite everything that has happened in the past thirteen years, God reconfirms his covenant with Abram. The Bible says that Abram falls on his face. It is here that God touches Abram deep within and transitions him from one level of faith to a deeper level of faith. It is here that Abram hears God differently and receives God's promise to him in a place where he has not experienced God before. It is here that the promise is reestablished.

It is here that the Lord changes Abram's name to Abraham and establishes the promise in the covenant with the reiteration that Abraham shall be a father of all nations. God tells Abraham his wife's name shall no longer be Sarai, but shall be changed to Sarah, and she will have a son, and she will be the mother of nations. Sarah, who was way past childbearing age, laughs at the thought she will bear a son. Sometimes, things do appear to be impossible, but with God, all things are possible—Isaac was born to ninety-nine-year-old Sarah and hundred-year-old Abraham. You are never too old nor is it ever too late to receive God's blessings.

After all Abraham and Sarah have gone through, from the time they left his father's house, God's blessings are starting to unfold in Abraham's life. Then God tests Abraham's faith by asking him to sacrifice his and Sarah's long-awaited son. It is the ultimate test of faith; and Abraham is willing to do it without hesitation. But then God steps in; Abraham looks up, and he sees his provision—God has given him a ram in the bush. Here's what I need you to understand: Abraham never doubted.

Take a lesson from Abraham and trust God's word before

- your promotion is announced;

- a financial breakthrough hits your bank account;

- your healing takes place;

- you meet your spouse;

- your spouse gets saved;

- your marriage is restored;

- your wayward child comes home and gets saved;

- the legal matter is resolved;

- the depression is lifted;

- you start looking for your new house.

Speak it in faith, trust that God will work it out for you, and believe it shall be so. For faith is the substance of things hoped for, and the evidence of things not seen. In fact, faith negates what we see in the natural. No matter what you're going through, you must trust God's promises in your life and hold on to God's word.

Just like God intervened in the nick of time for Abraham, God will intervene for you also. Just like Abraham, you must be willing to always put God first and keep focused on the promise. You must never allow anyone or anything to be above God in your life or to make you question the veracity of God's promises to you.

God blessed Abraham and Sarah, he gave them the desires of their hearts, and he fulfilled his promise, because God saw Abraham had his priorities in order and Abraham had an unshakable faith.

Look up and see God's provision in your life. That thing you've been praying for, that thing you have been waiting for—look up and there it shall be. When you look up, the check you've been waiting for will arrive in the mail. When you look up, your promotion and raise will be announced. When you look up, your estranged child will knock at your front door. Whatever you are in need of, when you look up, you will see God's provision. God has the resources to provide everything you need.

I know this is true because God has provided for me. I've been hungry, homeless, unemployed, sick, and lonely, but God worked it out. I am a living witness that God will do more than you could ever think or imagine when you look up. The Lord will work it out for you too. Just trust him, try him, depend on him, and lean on him. God will work it out. Stop worrying and start believing. If God did it before, God will do it again.

The remarkable thing about Abraham's blessing is, even though it occurred thousands of years ago, it was a generational promise. I know it's hard for you to apply what happened way back then, when the situation you're facing is happening in the here and now. So I want to share my generational blessing testimony with you to encourage you.

My grandmother had a sixth-grade education and she raised seven children. My mother was next to the youngest. She was the first to go to college, a historically black college in Austin, Texas. She didn't finish college, but years later, she had a daughter who would.

I grew up in Cambridge, Massachusetts. I went to elementary school and then to Cambridge High Latin. I was one of the few black students who were college prep students, yet, because I was one of the few black students, I never saw a counselor. No one in that school helped me decide what my next step after high school should be. During my sophomore year, I scored the highest grade on the English department exam. I didn't know how well I'd done until a brand new teacher took me outside of the classroom and whispered my accomplishment to me. She admonished me not to disclose the information to anyone.

After I graduated, I attended a career and finishing school. After that, I got a job working for the Cambridge Redevelopment Authority, which was a federally funded organization. (They were attempting to diversify the workplace.) But the Holy Ghost kept on churning in my spirit, and the Lord said to me, "Go back to school. You can go to Brandeis University or Boston University."

I ended up getting a job at Boston University in the Martin Luther King Center. Less than a year later, the director, Dr. Lawrence Carter, told me about a federal program that recruited African American students to attend Boston University. One of the twenty-one students who were enrolled in the program had dropped out. He asked, "Are you still interested in attending Boston University?"

He told me to go and see Mr. Grigsby in the admissions office. I prayed as I walked to Mr. Grigsby's office. Mr. Grigsby said to me, "Jo Ann, tell me about yourself and about your education." I told him everything. He said, "Okay. How were your grades?" I replied, "They were good." All of this occurred late on a Friday afternoon. I didn't take the trolley that day; instead I walked home from Boston to Cambridge praying to God. "God, you will work it out. God, I know you will. I know you can work it out."

When I arrived at work on Monday morning Dr. Carter told me to go down and see Mr. Grigsby. I walked to his office where he handed me my admissions letter to Boston University without a transcript or SAT scores. I was the culmination of the promise. My grandmother did not go to college; my mother started but did not finish. I was the beginning of the promise being fulfilled. Today, my daughter Candace has a bachelor's degree from Hampton University, and she's working on her master's at Howard; and my son is a Morehouse graduate. God will work it out. There is nothing too hard for God when you trust and believe.

While you are waiting for God to move in your situation, I'd like to leave you with five considerations that will edify you as you wait.

1. *Be patient.* You must be patient while you're waiting for your blessing to be manifested. Resist the temptation to "help" God in your situation. Trust that things will happen for you exactly when they are supposed to occur. Life is a journey and a process. Are you willing to wait until your promise is birthed into reality? What constructive things will you do in the meantime?

2. *Recall the things God has already done.* Is there anything too hard for God? Hasn't God made provisions for you in the past? It's easy to forget how much God has done for you when you are facing an

impending crisis. Take a moment to reflect on the ways God has come through for you throughout your life.

3. *Trust that God is working it out.* God is at work in your circumstance. It doesn't matter what area of your life is being impacted: your health, your employment status, your family, your finances, or your mind. You must develop an assurance deep down in your soul that God will work it out. God wants to work it out for you.

4. *Get your priorities straight.* Once your priorities are straight, God will fulfill the promise God spoke to you and God give you the very desires of your heart. Never allow others to be above God in your life. Not your spouse, not your children, not your job—God must come first.

5. *Don't taint your blessings.* If you're tired of waiting for God to bless you with a spouse, and you've made the decision to pursue someone else's spouse, you must stop now. If you're being considered for a promotion at work because you unfairly discredited a colleague, you need to make it right. If you've just signed a loan for a house, car, etc. that you know will end in financial disaster, you know you're out of sync. Get honest with yourself and with God. Any blessings that you gain by telling a lie will not last. Make a pledge to yourself and God to make it right while you are waiting for your breakthrough.

CHAPTER 6

A SONG FOR HOPE IN TRANSFIGURED REALITY

Elizabeth Mitchell Clement

Read: Pericope: Matthew 17:1–9, Matthew 17:7

Sing: "Over my head, I hear music in the air. Over my head, I hear music in the air. There must be a God somewhere!"

The air must have been thick coming down the mountain. Peter, James and John ought to have been pretty shaken up after their experience on that mountain with Jesus. I expect they may have taken a severe blow to their equilibrium; their status quo had been shattered.

Today, this is what we would call "cognitive dissonance"—a kind of psychological wind shear in which competing realities meet with such force they slice right through what makes sense. Airplanes cannot stay aloft in wind shear. Most people cannot, either. Think about it—these guys have been frightened out of their wits. After what they saw, can you blame them?

Under the circumstances, we would counsel them to talk about it; talk it through to make sense of what just happened. We might even tell them to reorientate their lives; the disorienting experience is helped by dialogue.

But Jesus has told them to tell no one.

As one who is extremely verbal, you should know, I have never understood this scripture. I must trust there is a good reason for this instruction that I do not yet comprehend, but my heart goes out to these poor guys. Don't you think they are dying to talk about it? I can overhear their imaginary conversation: "Was it just me? Did *you* see what I saw?"

"Are you *kidding* me? What *was* that?"

The air must have been thick coming down the mountainside. Nothing would ever be the same. They couldn't go back to the way it was before, and the way it would be hadn't come yet. They had entered a transfigured reality. What can hold us together in transfigured reality? Well, what if they had a song to sing?

Sing: "I will trust in the Lord. I will trust in the Lord. I will trust in the Lord, till I die. I will trust in the Lord. I will trust in the Lord. I will trust in the Lord, till I die. I don't know what just happened to me, but, I will trust in the Lord, till I die."

Dr. Bernice Johnson Reagon, one of the original SNCC (Student Nonviolent Coordinating Committee) Freedom Singers and founder of the a cappella ensemble Sweet Honey in the Rock, might call this transfigured reality "the change space." She tells a story about being a young freedom fighter in the 1960s. She says the jailhouse was a change space. Along with hundreds of other students, she was in jail because she and other Freedom Riders had caught a glimpse of a vision of a desegregated bus station and equal right for all Americans. As frightened as the Freedom Riders surely were, and in fear for their lives, they would not go back to where they had been, but where they were going was not there yet. Dr. Reagon called this the change space. We could call it "transfigured reality."

In her research as a historian and recalling those times, Professor Reagon asked the questions: "What holds you in the change space? What resources can you draw from?" The answer for those young people who bore within them a transfigured world was this—a song. They sang a song of hope in the change space.

In the chapter entitled "The Singing Movement," former Ambassador Rev. Andrew Young writes about young Bernice Reagon and the reorienting power of song in his civil rights memoir *An Easy Burden*:

> We found an uncut diamond among the Albany students in sixteen-year-old Bernice Johnson. During our first evening session [of the Dorchester citizenship training program], she and Rutha Harris and some of the other students started to sing. It seemed as if all the kids could sing, but Bernice's voice was as rich

as the soil around Albany, with the texture of all the suffering of black folk that made the crops grow . . . . Somehow through the music a great secret was discovered: that black people . . . could transcend (every difficulty) and forge a new determination, a new faith and strength, when fortified by song.

What do you have to keep you fortified in the change space? The movement's answer was to sing. They discovered, Reagon says, if you "run a song through your body, you have access to energy not available before."

Sing: "I woke up this morning with my mind stayed on Jesus. Woke up this morning with my mind, stayed on Jesus. Woke up this morning with my mind, stayed on Jesus. Hallelu, hallelu, hallelujah!"

Peter, James, and John needed a song to sing as they came down from their mountaintop experience. In singing, our young pioneers of justice discovered that a song helps to extend your capacity to endure what happens to you.

The power of singing that the Freedom Riders came upon was not their invention. The songs that adapted so well to their chaotic moment were old songs. They were the spirituals and "gospel pearls" they had learned in their many mostly rural churches.

The songs that could hold them in jail or as they came down the mountain were songs they knew by heart, songs that were lifted from their body memory. They were songs passed down from others who had known grief, indignity, fear, and uncertainty too strong for ordinary utterance. Singing transfigures the change space; singing makes it bearable and, perhaps, fruitful.

When the county sheriff forbid organizers to talk about voting rights and equal access to accommodations in the Albany Movement, they hummed until he left the building, then they sang about that transfigured world. The three disciples needed to sing! Jesus told them not to tell anyone what they had seen, but he didn't tell them they couldn't sing.

Isn't that why we come to church, to sing? Don't we go to church to lift our songs about the transfigured world of God's good news in Christ Jesus? Every time we worship and pray and tell these old stories over again, we enter the change space to sing our parts in God's transfiguring vision of the world. Every week, the invocation and call to worship invites us to this world not only as it is, but as it is in the dreams of God's own heart.

Every time we glimpse that vision of shalom, of justice, of a peace-filled world, we are in the change space. Every time God is glorified in our music, or the voices of children, or instruments, or the seasonal banners, we are in the change space, harkening the transfigured world. Every Lenten season, when we assume an attitude of reflection and repentance, we do so knowing on a Friday soon and the coming Easter morning, we will again see the agony of the cross transfigured in the glory of the resurrection. And we will sing "Hallelujah!" once again.

At the table of Holy Communion, we practice the transfigured world where everyone is welcome to share the bread of heaven, to feast until they want no more.

Sing: "Let us break bread together on our knees; let us break bread together on our knees. When I fall on my knees, with my face to the rising sun, My God, have mercy on me."

We know another young woman who sang her way through the change space. Her name was Mary and she was about sixteen years old when she sang her song. When the angel Gabriel announced to her that she would bear the presence of the Creator within her, a song welled up within her. It, too, was an old song. It was the song of her foremother Hannah but adapted to her transfigured reality. "My soul doth magnify the Lord," she sang (Luke 1:46 KJV). Her Magnificat—Mary's Song of Praise—was a song of hope for transfigured reality.

Sing: "My soul gives glory to my God. My heart pours out its praise. God lifted up my lowliness in many marvelous ways. Praise God, whose loving covenant supports those in distress, remembering past promises with present faithfulness."

For Mary, young Bernice, and for us, the old songs can hold us in hope in the change space, to give us strength to bear a transfigured reality into the world coming down the mountain.

Sing: "Over my head, I hear music in the air. Over my head, I hear music in the air. There must be a God somewhere!"

Amen.

CHAPTER 7

WHAT'S IN YOUR HOUSE?
Kingdom Women Embracing Our Abundance
Marie Murphy Phillips Braxton

Read: 2 Kings 4:1–7, 2 Kings 4:2 NIV

As I have grown older and prayerfully wiser, I have come to realize that if I were to believe everything I hear, read, and what I think I see, I would be, if you will pardon the expression—"twisted."

Daily, we are presented with so many lies, half-truths, contradictions, persuasions, and contentions that if you are not careful, you'll end up so messed up, you'll have no point of reality, no personal identity, or what is even worse, you'll have nothing on which to stand—no foundation! You will find yourself embracing a life of chaos, rather than embracing a genuine and fulfilling life of abundance.

In other words, there are too many people telling you too many different things. Stuff has gotten in the way; your mind is cluttered, there's too much noise, too many distractions; yet through it all, you claim you want to embrace your abundance! You think it's there (you want it to be), but you just haven't been able to quite get your arms around it—your abundance.

There's a story in 2 Kings that tells of an unnamed woman who could have very well been you—if you have ever been in a situation that appeared to be hopeless.

The story is told in chapter 4 in just seven short verses. The woman's husband has died and she is left with their two young sons. We know that they are young and underage because they are referred to as "boys." They were youngsters, which meant they were too young to work to support her. None of the males in her deceased husband's family had offered to marry her, as was customary in the Jewish tradition, so she was left to rear her sons by herself.

The story opens with the woman going to Elisha, the priest who succeeded Elijah. She desperately cried, telling him that her husband's creditor was coming to take her sons away and force them into slavery as payment for her husband's debt.

Oh, can't you hear yourself crying out, "I can't pay my rent, so I'm going to be evicted. I can't pay my car note, so it's going to be repossessed. I can't pay my mortgage, so my home will go into foreclosure. I'm going to lose my job because of the sequester. I'm going through a divorce, one of my children is in jail, and another is on drugs. I'm about to lose my mind! It took every dime and every bit of strength I could muster to be where I am today and you talk about embracing my abundance!"

The woman's young sons were on the verge of being sold into slavery. Our mothers of generations past endured the pain of having their young sons and daughters snatched from their arms. They wept and they wailed—the children were sold on auction blocks like livestock . . . never to be seen again except in their mother's mind's eye, dreams, and imaginings.

Elisha, the priest answers, "How can I help you?"

Like the unnamed woman, you cry to God and God asks, "How can I help you?" You say, "I want my abundance that I might embrace it."

Elisha replied to the woman as I believe God is replying to you right now, "*What do you have in your house?*"

You say, "God, I want to embrace my abundance" and in my heart I hear God saying, "Well, there needs to be something there to embrace."

The term *abundance* is a noun that refers to a person, place, thing, or idea. Is your abundance something that is tangible or is it something you cannot see but you know is there? Is your understanding of *abundance* a closet filled with designer clothes and stiletto heels with red soles, or is your understanding of *abundance* that which overflows from a God-centered, full, and satisfying life?

Elisha asks the unnamed woman, "What's in your house?" She answers without hesitation, "Nothing." The NIV translation says, "Your servant has nothing there at all."

Beloved, if you want to embrace your abundance, I would suggest you look at what is in your house. I'm not talking about your physical house, but your spiritual house. Take a look around. Is it empty, void of what makes for a life of abundance that you can hold on to, a life of abundance that you can wrap your arms around?

As I shared in the beginning of this sermon, we hear so many conflicting messages, lies, and half-truths, and there's so much noise and chatter going on in our minds that we don't know what to believe. You see, some will tell you, you can have it all—everything you've ever wanted: from a mansion on a hill, Bentley in your four-car garage (even if you don't have a job!), to having all your bills paid and your cares and concerns taken away. All you need do is say "Jesus" and it's yours for the asking. But I want you to know that although Jesus does say, "Ask and it will be given to you," the Bible neither mentions nor teaches that simply calling the Lord's name will give you all the stuff you want for your abundance.

Is your spiritual house empty? If so, now is the time to start filling it with the essential elements of your abundance.

Elisha asks the woman what she has in her house and she answers "nothing." She then remembers, however, that she has a little oil. (Pause for a minute; we'll come back to the story.)

Your spiritual house may be empty; however, within you and all creation is God's spirit. God, who created every living being, breathed into his spirit. In the Old Testament the oil represented the anointing of the Spirit of God. God's life-giving spirit is in your house, but you need more in order to embrace your abundance.

Make a list so you don't leave anything out.

First and foremost, you absolutely must love God with all your heart, with all your mind, and with all your soul. Your love for God in Christ Jesus must be at the center of your being—at the very core of your existence. It must take precedence over every person, every thing, every desire, every wish, and every dream. You cannot help but love God who loved you so much that he gave his only son, Jesus, to die on the cross for your sins so that you would not die but have everlasting life. You love God so much that you praise, worship, pray, witness, and serve God.

Do you want to embrace your abundance? Then start thanking God for what God has already done for you. Thank God for what you already have. Thank God for saving you and giving you new life, a new song, a new reason for living!

What's in your house? In your house is your love for God in Christ Jesus our Lord and Savior, but also there is the love of your brothers and sisters, who are children of God.

There needs to be some faith in your spiritual house. Faith is belief. In the book of Romans it says "faith is the substance of things hoped for, the evidence of things not seen." You've never seen God but you believe that God is God in Jesus Christ. You have faith and believe that God is able to do all things exceedingly well. Faith in God means you trust God in every situation.

You want to embrace your abundance? Well, what's in your house, your spiritual house? You have the life-giving Spirit of God or the breath of God, and you have love and faith. But there are some other things too. You need to have joy that rings on the inside, joy that makes your soul happy even when there is nothing but sadness and despair all around. You need peace, peace that passes the understanding of this world, peace that brings calm in the midst of a storm.

There needs to be patience that keeps you intact when the wrong buttons have been pushed, kindness that extends beyond just those who do kind things for you, goodness for the sake of Jesus, faithfulness you can depend upon, even when it's inconvenient, gentleness that will enable you to be tender without being a pushover, and self-control so you may exercise self-discipline at all times.

Back to the story. Elisha asks the woman what she has in her house. She says nothing but a little oil. He then tells her to go to all her neighbors and collect jars, and not just a few. When she's done, she is to bring them into her house and close the door.

The analogy here could very well mean that God wants you to bring into your spiritual house only those things that are according to God's will. God will abundantly bless you, but don't clutter your spiritual house with a whole lot of junk God cannot use. *Be careful of what you bring into your house!* It's that other stuff that may block your ability to embrace your abundance.

Close the door. Keep the lies, deceptions, confusion, conflicts, hatred, half-truths, distractions, and anything else that might prevent you from embracing your abundance on the other side of the door. *Your spiritual house is your sanctuary. Treat it with reverence and respect.*

The woman does as Elisha, the man of God, tells her. She closes the door behind her. She closes her mind to the troubles of the world and the troubles she's going through.

After she closes the door, she pours the oil into each container. When each is full, she sets it aside. She may not understand what is going on, but she pours the oil. She keeps pouring, filling each container.

She pours. Oh, can't you hear David singing his psalm, "He anointeth my head with oil, my cup runneth over?"

She pours. Oh, can't you see Malachi writing these words, "He will open up the windows of heaven and pour out a blessing you cannot contain?"

She pours. Oh, can't you testify with Paul, "My God will supply all your needs according to his riches in glory"?

She pours. "The Lord is my Shepherd, I have everything I need."

She pours. "Jehovah Jira, my Provider. Jehovah Nice, you reign in victory."

She pours. "With God, all things are possible."

She pours. "I have come that you might have life and have it more abundantly."

She pours until there are no more containers to fill.

"Go, sell the oil, pay your husband's debt, and you and your sons shall live on what is left over."

What is left to be said?

"Now to him who is able to do immeasurably more than all we ask or imagine, according to his power that is at work within us, to him be glory in the church and in Christ Jesus throughout all generations, for ever and ever! Amen."

CHAPTER 8

WHAT YOU HAVE . . . IS MORE THAN ENOUGH!

Cheryl A. Lindsay

Read: John 6:1–21

Leftovers. Leftovers are interesting. They are remnants. Some may say scraps. Others call them discards. But they are what is left over after a meal has been consumed . . . after all have eaten their fill . . . satisfied their appetites . . . and are now ready to push back from the table.

Sometimes we get leftovers because we've prepared too much. Sometimes we get leftovers because what we've made really wasn't all that good. Other times, we end up with leftovers intentionally. We planned the meal that way. We made enough for this meal plus a little extra for another time or for an entirely different meal, so we knew when we started we would end up with something to spare.

Interesting—this is what our text is about. One of Jesus' most famous miracles was the feeding of the five thousand. After all have had their fill, Jesus is concerned with making sure his disciples had collected the leftovers. It's interesting because Jesus isn't necessarily known for being concerned with holding on. This is the same Jesus who called the disciples away from their homes and trades. "Follow me," he told them, and they did, leaving the lives they had behind. This is the same Jesus who sent his disciples to perform miracles, to heal the sick, to feed the hungry, to cast out demons, to do all the things he had done. Jesus told them to take nothing for their journey, to even shake the dust off their feet when they left a town. So what's the deal with picking up the scraps after this particular meal? Why were these leftovers so important?

Jesus had been teaching. A crowd had gathered around him as news of his healing miracles spread. After his teaching, it was time to eat, but rather than dismiss the people to find their own meal, Jesus turned to one of his disciples with a question. And the question became a test.

Have you ever found yourself doing exactly what you knew God wanted you to do but still found yourself facing incredible obstacles at the same time? Have you had the experience of making the decision to follow Jesus and then found that life suddenly got a little harder when you thought it would be easier? You do what you're supposed to do but you have not yet experienced the blessings you expected to come along with your behavior. Maybe Jesus is testing you. Maybe Jesus wants to know if you will still trust him when: you fasted and prayed but still look for answers; you're in Bible study but you still deal with relationship problems; you're tithing but still struggling financially. Will you be like Job and say, "Though he may slay, yet will I trust him?" Will you continue to trust God with the plan even when God doesn't let you in on the plan?

Surely, there is a plan. We do not serve an arbitrary God. We serve a God who is intentional and specific. Jesus knew what he was going to do to feed the multitude on the mountain, and Jesus knows what he's going to do in your situation. But will you trust him even when you can't see or even imagine what he's up to? Sometimes we block our own blessing because we focus on the seemingly overwhelming task *before* us instead of focusing on the all-powerful God who is *with* us.

The disciples focused on their lack. Phillip said six months wages couldn't do it. What was unsaid was that neither disciple had a penny. They thought they had nothing, but after looking around they were able to come up with something. Sometimes you just have to take a little inventory to see what you have before you say it's not possible. Check the cupboard; you may not have what you want but you probably have something. Open the refrigerator. You may not have a taste for what you see but you probably have something. Look at your bank account. You may feel like you're down to your last dime but you probably can come up with a couple of dollars. Your friends may not return your calls but you can find somebody to talk to. Even when it seems like there's nothing, God is going to provide something.

Our job is to take stock and recognize what we have even when it comes in a way or from a source we don't expect. Andrew says, "There is a boy here." Understand, when the five thousand were counted, only men were counted. There were also women and children there but they were not included in the count. So the source of the seed of this miracle—the one who came prepared with a meal, the little boy, was not counted. He was too young to be included in the number. Sometimes we block our blessing because it may come packaged in a way we cannot accept.

What can they tell us? They're too young. They haven't lived enough yet. What can they tell us? They're too old and the world has passed them by. You can't tell me about my marriage because you're single. You can't tell me about dating because you've been married for twenty years. You're too tall. You're too short, too fat, or too thin. You don't have any money. You have too much money. You're too holy. You're not holy enough. You talk too much. You don't talk enough. We block our blessing because we get caught up with our preconceived notions of who and what God will use to bless us. But if we can just free our minds, we will realize God can use whomever and whatever God chooses to use to bring about God's blessings.

So now the disciples have taken inventory and they have something. It doesn't seem to be enough, but they have something. What they have, they presented to Jesus. I don't know what you have but you have something, and whatever that something is, you need to give it to Jesus. When you give what you have to Jesus, Jesus will magnify and multiply your "something" into abundance. We don't know how many loaves and fishes Jesus produced that day but we do know five thousand—or maybe ten to fifteen thousand—men, women, and children ate all they wanted and were satisfied.

Jesus didn't give them just enough; he magnified what they had because that's the God we serve. Jesus didn't give them a snack. He gave them a full meal. He didn't stave off their hunger; he left them satisfied. When you turn over what you have to Jesus, just watch and see Jesus magnify your "something" into everything. Watch Jesus supply all your needs according to his riches. Watch Jesus do abundantly and exceedingly above anything you could ask or think. Watch Jesus open up the windows of heaven and pour out an overflowing blessing into your life and into your situation.

Our God is a God of plenty and abundance and generosity. Consider this: the people hadn't asked for anything. Most miracles came after someone approached Jesus with their need. The woman with the issue of blood who crawled through the crowd just to touch him, Jairus, the ruler of the synagogue who humbled himself and asked a carpenter to lay hands on his daughter so she would be well, the men who cut a hole in the roof of a house so their friend would be healed, the blind man who received the ability to see, the lame man who was given the ability to walk, the leper whose skin was healed. All came to Jesus with their concern. This crowd had assembled because they had heard about Jesus' healing power. Therefore, we can imagine a fair number of them were sick or cared for someone who was sick. Jesus realized they had an immediate need of which they were unaware to ask him about. They didn't know Jesus could feed five thousand-plus people with one family's rations, but Jesus knew what he could do for them—just like he knows what he can do for you.

So Jesus has the disciples tell the crowd to sit. The text said those who were seated got to eat. Jesus knew the people had to be hungry. They didn't have to ask him. Remember, Jesus already knew what he was going to do. Jesus didn't tell them to sit down, he told the disciples to tell them. I wonder how many people walked away hungry and had to search for food because they refused to listen to Jesus' messengers. We do know more than five thousand were filled and satisfied because they were obedient to the men of God even when it didn't make sense. They did what God instructed through God's messengers, and God honored their obedience. Don't think that only the apostles were being tested. Don't think that Jesus stopped being in the testing business that day on the beach. Today, some of us know God still honors obedience to those who honor God's instructions as delivered through God's messengers. Some of us know what it is to do something because of obedience.

With joy and gratitude out of the abundance of God's generosity, some of us give of our time, talent, and treasure. Others write a check out of obedience. Yes, God loves a cheerful giver, but God blesses them all. Let's be real, sometimes it's easy to do what God says to do, especially when we can see the benefit, when it's what we've asked for, when it's fun, when we get recognized for it, when we get something out of it, and when we have a reasonable understanding of how God is working. There are times, however, when we say, "Okay, Lord, if that's what you want." Sometimes there's no enthusiasm, no joy. "But if you want me to sit here, I'll sit down here with thousands of people waiting to be fed even though all I can see is a few loaves of bread and a couple of fish. I don't know what you're doing, but if you say sit down, I'll sit down. I'll watch you work and I'll receive what you have for me." That's what the multitude did that day and God blessed them. They ate until they were full and satisfied. But Jesus still wasn't done.

Jesus told the disciples, gather what's left, and when they did, they had more than when they started. They thought they had nothing and found they had something. After God had satisfied them, they had more leftovers than the original meal. Someone may think that's all well and say, "I've been to the cupboard and the cupboard is bare. I have gone to my car and the fuel tank is on empty and the ignition will not start. My bank accounts are depleted and my retirement is gone. My family has turned their back on me and my so-called friends cannot be found. I don't just feel like I have something. I've done my inventory and I still have nothing."

I want you to know, if you have breath in your body you have something. Sometimes all you may have is your praise. But if you will take your praise and give that praise to Jesus, Jesus will magnify and multiply it, leaving you with more than enough. Sometimes when you feel lost and alone, all you have is the memory of that favorite children's song, "Jesus loves me, this I know, for the Bible tells me so . . ."

What you have is more than enough! Sometimes when you feel burdened by bad choices, poor decisions, past mistakes, and tough breaks, all you have is "amazing grace, how sweet the sound, that saved a wretch like me. I once was lost but now am found, was blind but now I see." What you have is more than enough! Sometimes when you don't know where to turn or what to do, all you have is "blessed assurance, Jesus is mine. Oh what a foretaste of glory divine. Heir of salvation, purchase of God, born in his spirit washed in his blood." What you have is more than enough! If all you have is "thank you, Jesus," what you have is more than enough! If all you have is "to God be the glory," what you have is enough! If all you have is "you are great. You do miracles so great," what you have is more than enough! If all you have is "stand still and know that he is God," what you have is more than enough!

When you think you have nothing, look around. You will find you have something. When you take something and put that something into God's hands, trust and believe God already knows what God is going to do. God will multiply your something and magnify it so not only will you be satisfied, not only will you have all you want, not only will you be full, you're going to have some leftovers. God is going to fix this thing so you'll have more leftovers than you started with. What you have is more than enough!

CHAPTER 9

CUT IT OFF AND CUT IT LOOSE!

Monica Hardy-McCray

Read: Hebrews 12:1 AMP Sermon Text: Mark 9:43–48 KJV

As I grow in God, I realize more and more how dangerous the flesh really is. I'm not just talking about the obvious or physical acts of flesh—I'm talking about being more careful with what I say, what I see, what I hear, what I think, what I smell, what I taste, where I go, whom I go with, how I act, and how I react.

Yes, God created us in God's image, but the five senses that God gave us are related to our flesh, not our faith. As a matter of fact, we often miss God because we lack faith, and "without faith it is impossible to please God." Instead, we would rather see, hear, smell, or touch—"Now faith is the substance of things hoped for and the evidence of things *not seen.*" Simply put, yet thought provoking, our time on earth is short! Therefore, we should stop and take inventory of our lives and assess whether or not what we are doing is honoring God. Start with your flesh, because flesh is not your friend!

Let's look at the definition of three key words: *Cut* means to sever, slice, chop, hack, slash, incise, carve, amputate, and disunite. Break means to sever something or separate a part of something. *Temptation* means to lure, entice, attract, excite, persuade, pull, or induce. It is a desire or craving for something, especially something considered wrong (it's usually something you really want deep down anyway). *Justification* is an explanation, validation, rationalization, or excuse. It is a reason or circumstance that justifies an action or attitude. *If you fail to cut it off and cut it loose, you may be tempted, and once you give in to temptation, you will justify it!*

Hebrews 12:1 says, "*Therefore then, since we are surrounded by so great a cloud of witnesses [who have borne testimony to the Truth], let us strip off and throw aside every encumbrance (unnecessary weight) and that sin which so readily (cleverly) clings to and entangles us, and let us run with patient endurance and steady and active persistence the appointed course of the race that is set before us.*" As believers, we have a race to run. This race is arranged by God according to God's word and through examples of faithful servants who have gone before us. The apostle urges the Hebrews to a two-fold duty: *Prepare* means to cut it off and cut it loose (trim the fat and/or excess) because there are some sins that cling to us and will eventually entangle us, and *perfect* means to cultivate (grow) your faith and patience. *If we were to be honest, oftentimes we give in to flesh and sin because we have no faith and no patience*!

Mark 9:43–48 says: "*If your hand causes you to sin, cut it off. It is better for you to enter life maimed than with two hands to go into hell, where the fire never goes out. And if your foot causes you to sin, cut it off. It is better for you to enter life crippled than to have two feet and be thrown into hell. And if your eye causes you to sin, pluck it out. It is better for you to enter the kingdom of God with one eye than to have two eyes and be thrown into hell, where 'their worm does not die, and the fire is not quenched.'*" Remember it's not about you! So if it gets in God's way, get rid of it. If it distracts you, impairs you, or limits you, get rid of it! According to God's word, when you see Jesus you will be made whole!

Let's explore other related scripture text. Genesis 39:12 (KJV) reads, "*And she caught him by his garment, saying, lie with me; and he left his garment in her hand, and fled, and got him out.*" When it comes to your flesh, it is in your best interest to *flee* or run away to escape temptation. Matthew 26:41 (KJV) says: "*Watch and pray, that ye enter not into temptation: the spirit indeed is willing, but the flesh is weak.*" Have you ever found yourself in a situation because you were not watchful or prayerful or you took a person or situation for granted? Sooner or later, you realized you were not strong enough to handle the situation you were in. An important lesson to learn is, if God delivered you from drinking, don't work at a bar. If God delivered you from fornication, don't invite your friend to your home; go out on a date. If God delivered you from smoking, then stop hanging around smokers or sitting near the smoking section. If God delivered you from stealing, don't work around money.

1 Corinthians 15:31–34 (NIV) says: *"I face death every day—yes, just as surely as I boast about you in Christ Jesus our Lord. If I fought wild beasts in Ephesus with no more than human hopes, what have I gained? If the dead are not raised, 'Let us eat and drink, for tomorrow we die.' Do not be misled: 'Bad company corrupts good character.'"* Come back to your senses and stop sinning, for there are some who are ignorant of God. I say this to your shame. Here the apostles are giving a caution against people with loose lives and principles. If there were no resurrection, we could just live and act like beasts. In order to keep innocence, you must keep good company. Error is infectious. It's time to think wisely. Awaken to the holiness of life. Ignorance of God is a luxury that no one can afford.

Leviticus 20:3–7 (NIV) says: *"The LORD said to Moses, 'I myself will set my face against him and will cut him off from his people; for by sacrificing his children to Molek, he has defiled my sanctuary and profaned my holy name. If the members of the community close their eyes when that man sacrifices one of his children to Molek and if they fail to put him to death, I myself will set my face against him and his family and will cut them off from their people together with all who follow him in prostituting themselves to Molek. . . . I will set my face against anyone who turns to mediums and spiritists to prostitute themselves by following them, and I will cut them off from their people. . . . Consecrate yourselves and be holy, because I am the LORD your God. Keep my decrees and follow them. I am the LORD, who makes you holy.* If God is willing to CUT people or things OFF then why aren't you? In order to cut off and cut loose, you must consecrate (separate) yourself. Limit and give up things that your flesh desires so you can strengthen your spirit. You must be *holy* in all your actions and conversations. If you make your tree good, the fruit will be good!

Today, many people who are *saved are also stuck.* The reason why they are stuck is because they cut off their problem; however, they didn't cut their problem loose. In other words, they stop doing "it" but didn't detach from "it!" Sin is still dangling around, lying and waiting like residue or soap scum after cleaning. To specify, you stopped calling but kept the phone number, you said I accept your apology but kept the attitude, you stopped hanging out with them but keep calling them friends, you stopped dating but keep condoms in the drawer by the bed, you stopped the affair but you are still listening to "y'all's song," you stopped smoking but you kept the pipe, you said you did not care but you still talk about it, you stopped shopping (spending money) but you stay in the mall, and you stopped watching late night TV but you kept certain channels.

I simply told you to not only stop sinning but flee or get away from the things that caused or cause you to sin. Joshua 24:15 (NIV) says. *"But if serving the* LORD *seems undesirable to you, then choose for yourselves this day whom you will serve, whether the gods your ancestors served beyond the Euphrates, or the gods of the Amorites, in whose land you are living. But as for me and my household, we will serve the* LORD.*"* It's time to get saved for real! Figure out what's causing you to sin, cut it off and cut it loose, *then* turn from your wicked ways, *then* allow the spirit of God to have free course, and *then* your land will be healed. *Be bold enough to cut if off and cut it loose!*

CHAPTER 10

WHAT IS YOUR STORY?

Gwendolyn E. Boyd

Read: Acts 4:1–22

There is a word from the Lord. The scripture text is Acts 4:1-22. I, however, will share the verse for my focal pericope from *The Message Bible*, verses 5–8. It is as follows:

> *The next day a meeting was called in Jerusalem. The rulers, religious leaders, religion scholars, Annas the Chief Priest, Caiaphas, John, Alexander—everybody who was anybody was there. They stood Peter and John in the middle of the room and grilled them: "Who put you in charge here? What business do you have doing this?"*

"What's your story?" "Who put you in charge here?" Or as we like to say in the African American community, with attitude: "What's your story?" "Who do you think you are?" In other words, "Who died and put you in charge?"

Everybody has a story. Everywhere you go, especially in the Washington, DC, area, everybody wants to know who you are and "What's your story?" If you are at a reception and working the room, people want to know what company you are associated with, what corporation you are with, what firm you represent, where you practice, who your clients are, who you are and what you do. Why? Everybody has a story.

If you are at a conference, people who are supposed to be in the know—those who know everybody but may not be familiar with you—will want to know who you are and whether or not you are an

51

attendee, presenter, or speaker. In other words, what's your story? Why are you here? If you mix and mingle at a social event before you share the digits, the other person would want to know your story. What's your name? Where are you from? Where do you work? What make of car do you drive? And the most obnoxious question: How much do you bring home after taxes? Notice, they seldom ask where you worship. That, however, is another sermon for another time. People want to know, "What's your story?" Everybody has a story.

All of us construct narratives about ourselves—where we have come from and where we think we are going. Stories can take on many forms. We know some stories from our community. There are stories in our family and relatives who always have a story to tell. Most of the time, the stories are full of *drama!*

There are funny stories—some that are embarrassing personal stories, some that people repeat over and over and over again. Tall tales are made up to make a bad situation look good. There are stories that don't have a word of truth in them. "Girrrrrl, you did not hear it from me, but . . . ."

There are good and bad stories. We hear stories at the beauty salon, barbershop, and nail salon. We hear stories at the bus stop, on the train, in the car pool, and around the water cooler. Stories of fact and stories of pure fiction. We are familiar with stories about courage and strength. We have heard inspirational stories and we know of compelling stories.

There are stories that help us fill in the gaps in our history as African Americans. This is how Alex Haley was able to trace his roots. Stories had been passed down through generations in his family using the African tradition of the griot, or storyteller.

Everybody has a story. Stories define us. To know others well is to know their stories—the experiences that have shaped them, their trials, their struggles, and the turning points that have tested them on this journey we call life.

Everybody has a story. Professionally, we let our résumés tell our story—the story of our success and our achievements. Everybody has a story of special moments. Some of us have a pancake house story. Nevertheless, everybody has a story.

Some of us have a story of a situation or circumstance that defies logic or explanation. We have stories of miracles that have occurred in our lives or in the lives of our friends and loved ones. These are the stories of our faith. We call them our testimonies—stories that share the good news of what God has done and what God continues to do in our lives every day. These are the stories to inspire and encourage us: our testimony. These are the stories in which we remember the time we almost let go, but God kept us. These are the stories in which we remember the times we ate peanut—without the butter—and jelly sandwiches. But God fed us. These are the stories in which we could not pay our bills because the checkbook balance had insufficient funds. But God paid our bills.

There are stories in which you received a negative report from your doctor. But you fell on your face before the Lord and when you went back to the doctor, she said, "I don't understand it, but the tumor is gone." "The spot on your lung is gone." "The infection is gone." God was faithful to God's word that by Jesus' stripes we are healed.

There are stories in which God gave you a new yet better job where you made more money than you had ever seen in your life. There are stories in which they said you would not qualify for the house that you now live in or the car you now drive.

There are stories in which they told you to give up. There are stories in which you would were told that you could never have children and now your children are running around, driving you crazy.

There are stories in which they said you would not go to college but you graduated summa cum laude. There are stories in which they gave you a pink slip, or came in your office and closed the door. You were blindsided and left with unpaid bills, not enough money, and no job to provide for your family. Every job application you submitted, you were told you were overqualified, or they could use you but not pay you what you are really worth. You almost threw in the towel. You almost gave up. And that is when God stepped in!

There are stories in which you wanted to start your own business and could not get the loan. You had no collateral. God stepped in and said, "I will supply all your needs according to my riches in glory."

There are stories in which your case was coming up and looked hopeless, but God stepped in and the case was dismissed. There are stories in which you were physically, financially, and emotionally attacked. God stepped in.

What's your story? Everybody has a story to tell. The book of

Acts records the activities and the stories of the disciples and tells the story of the birth and expansion of the church. The author of Acts, traditionally identified as Luke, the physician, provides the sequel to the Jesus story. He tells about the words and deeds of Jesus and provides the details of the activities of the apostles.

The plot line of Acts begins with the ascension of Jesus, shares the birth of the church energized by the Spirit, and continues with the spread of the gospel to the ends of the earth. In chapter 4, we find Peter and John being interrogated about the healing of the lame man in chapter 3 at the gate of temple called Beautiful. It is a familiar story. The man had been lame since birth and on this particular day he saw Peter and John going into the temple. As was the custom of the lame man, he asked them for alms. Their response, however, was not what the lame man or the crowd expected (Acts 3:6 KJV). *"Then Peter said, Silver and gold have I none; but such as I have give I thee; in the name of Jesus Christ of Nazareth rise up and walk."*

And so the plot thickens. Verse 1 of chapter 4 records that the priests, the chief of the Temple police, and some Sadducees came. They were indignant that these upstart apostles were proclaiming the resurrection story. So they arrested them. They threw them in jail. The next morning, they brought Peter and John before the Sanhedrin. In the text, we find Peter and John, on trial, being questioned.

The Message Bible version makes it plain in Acts 4:5–7:

> *The next day a meeting was called in Jerusalem. The rulers, religious leaders, religion scholars, Annas the Chief Priest, Caiaphas, John, Alexander—everybody who was anybody was there. They stood Peter and John in the middle of the room and grilled them: "Who put you in charge here? What business do you have doing this?"*

The apostles have to tell their story. They are cross-examined and given the third degree. They have to tell *their story*. They had to tell their story to those on the Sanhedrin Council who really didn't know or care who they were. The members of the Sanhedrin Council are annoyed by the message the apostles are sharing.

The apostles have to tell their story to those who thought they were "in charge of being in charge." First, I want to remind you that when you stand up for Jesus, you will be put to the test. When you stand up for what is right, they will call a meeting on you. They will try to stop you and block your progress and do everything they can to stand in your way. When you stand up for Jesus, folk will put you down. You will be laughed at, scorned, and ridiculed.

The Sanhedrin tried to put Peter and John on lock down. They were put to the test because of their testimony and their faith. If you find yourself willing to stand up for the Lord, you will be put to the test. Their faith was put on trial and tested in the Sanhedrin Council. The prosecutor brought forth the charges. "You men have been teaching and preaching the resurrection of Jesus from the dead." There was no defense attorney but we know that God showed up as their *lawyer in the courtroom.*

Let me remind you that you never know who you are until you are tried and tested in the courtroom of life. We can all come to church and say, "Praise the Lord!" when the worship leader says, "Praise the Lord!" What are you saying on your own time? The question is when the storms of life are raging in your life, is your soul anchored in the Lord? The true test is not what you do in calm waters; the true test is how you handle the storms in your life. If you have never had any storms, just keep on living.

The Sanhedrin took Peter and John, locked them up, and put them on trial. We need to understand one thing about this passage. The Sanhedrin were afraid of Peter and John's *ministry,* but they attacked the men. The Sanhedrin were afraid of the apostles' testimony, their gifts and talents, their teaching and their preaching—but they attacked the men. The Sanhedrin were afraid of the apostles' accomplishments, their promotions—but they attacked the men. The Sanhedrin were afraid of the apostles' anointing, their presence, and the power of the Holy Ghost in them—but they attacked the men. The Sanhedrin were afraid and worried about how far the apostles would go, how high they would climb, how blessed they would be, and what they would become. The Sanhedrin were afraid of the apostles' *ministry,* but they attacked the *men.* The Sanhedrin could not say the healing did not happen because the man was standing right there, so when they could not attack what the apostles had done, they attacked the men. The adversary wants to turn your attention away from what you are *doing*—to *self-preservation.* They make it personal.

You must understand that many of the personal attacks against you are occurring because others are afraid of the Christ in you, afraid of what God is doing in you and through you, and afraid of where God is getting ready to take you. Satan has seen your potential and wants to stop you before it goes too far. But you have to affirm in your spirit that no matter what it looks like, no matter how hard the battle, no matter how big the enemy, no matter how great the adversary, we are reminded of Romans 8:31, *"If God be for us, who can be against us?"* and Romans 8:37, *"Nay, in all these things we are more than conquerors through him that loved us."*

So when the smoke clears and the dust settles, you will still be here, you will still be standing on the promises of God. God's promises are "Yes" and "AMEN." You must also remember that when you work for God and do what is right, when you share your testimony and walk by faith and not by sight, be clear that the enemy knows if he can stop *you*, he can stop what is coming through you. This is why the attack is so strong.

You might be sitting at your desk, minding your business, and out of nowhere, BOOM! Be clear. The strategy of the adversary is to discredit *who you are*, not *what you do*. Your enemies will dig up dirt on you and if they cannot find anything, they will make it up. But God will always give you a sign that you are on the right track. Look for the signs that God is working through you.

God has promised us that "no weapon formed against us shall prosper." It may be formed but it will not prosper. Even if they dig a ditch for you and throw you in it (Joseph's brothers), God will put a trampoline in the bottom of it so you will bounce back (out) and God will get the glory out of your testimony. God gets the glory when you tell your story about God's grace and mercy. This is important to know. "What others meant for evil, God will turn it into good." The text reminds us that the Sanhedrin tried to do Peter and John in, but in spite of the attack against God's messengers, they could not stop the *message,* and five thousand souls were saved.

No one could speak against the apostles. The men stood as evidence of the healing power of Jesus. Scripture recorded, "but with the man right before them, seeing him standing there so upright—so healed!" What could they say against that?

Second, since that did not work, the Sanhedrin Council tried another tactic. They said to Peter and John, you need to know that "we are in charge." You don't want to buck us because we represent authorized, elected, appointed authority. You think it is hard now? Keep talking about this Jesus and see what happens. Peter and John were threatened to try to make them conform to the Sanhedrin way of thinking, doing, and operating.

African Americans are all too familiar with those strategies. "You think it is hard now? You made it through the glass ceiling, and the rules change. You now have to make it through a concrete ceiling. African Americans are more than casually familiar with the connection between our struggles and our testimonies. We know the struggle we have come through as a people—from the Middle Passage through slavery, having to make bricks without straw, lynchings and church bombings, Jim Crow and segregation.

We have had to deal with Lester Maddox, George Wallace, Strom Thurmond, and Jesse Helms. We have watched them kill our leaders and brutalize our people. And even today, as we look at the issues we face in our community, we wonder what is wrong with this story. What is wrong with this story when we see we are still dealing with the issues of racial profiling? We are the last hired, first fired, and red-lined by banks. We are fighting a war we still don't understand—for freedom and justice—in a far-off land, when some of us don't have freedom and justice in our own country. Our children don't have access to the tools they need to get a quality education.

There are those who still question our intelligence, challenge our authority, and discount what we think, say, and do. ENOUGH is ENOUGH!!

Peter and John told the Sanhedrin, "You are ordinary authority. We serve a higher authority. We are not settling for your authority. We serve a God who has ALL power and authority." This is the confidence we as Christians must have today. This is the faith we must have to speak to the enemy. We must have confidence to say, "Devil, you should have killed me while you had a chance!" We are going to speak now more than ever before, as I have a story to tell. You want to know who died and put me in charge? "*Then Peter, filled with the Holy Ghost, said to them, 'Rulers of the people and elders, if we are questioned today because of a good deed done to someone who was sick and are asked how this man has been healed, let it be known to all of you, and to all the people of Israel, that this man is standing before you in good health by the name of Jesus Christ of Nazareth, whom you crucified, whom God raised from the dead* (Acts 4:8–10, NRSV). "You want to know by what power, or by what name, have we done this?" Peter said, "*There is salvation in no one else, for there is no other name under heaven given among mortals by which we must be saved* (Acts 4:12, NRSV).

I have a story to tell. You want to know who's in charge? The one whose death, burial, and resurrection was the pivotal event that split history into "before" and "after," and changed the world forevermore. You ask, how can we do this? And by what authority? The one Paul wrote about in his letter to the Philippians (2:9–11): "*Therefore God also highly exalted him and gave him the name that is above every name: so that at the name of Jesus every knee should bend, in heaven and on earth, and under the earth, and every tongue should confess that Jesus Christ is Lord, to the glory of God the Father.*" That's my story.

Finally, we have to know that when we speak out for the Lord, he will give us the courage to stand. If you read verse 15 (in *The Message*), it says it this way: "*They sent them (Peter and John) out of the room so they could work out a plan. They talked it over: 'What can we do with these men? By now it's known all over town that a miracle has occurred, and that they are behind it. There is no way we can refute that. But, so that it doesn't go any further, let's silence them with threats so they won't dare to use Jesus' name ever again with anyone.*'"

Whenever we are faced with these awesome moments, we have to remember who died and left us to tell the story. God will turn the situation around and make it work in your favor.

We must have a switch in us, because in moments of severe crises we are no match for the powers and principalities of this world. When times get real tough, we have to make a bold proclamation to the world: "*I am determined to stand.*" Stand up for what is right. Stand up as a follower of Christ and be not ashamed. Stand up for Christ and stop apologizing for it. Yes, God is using you and me. Yes, God is working on you and me. Yes, God is empowering you and me. Yes, God has God's hands on you and me. God will get the glory out of our lives.

God does not want us to be enthusiastic spectators in the kingdom. God wants us to take action. Daniel 11:32 says, "*But the people who are loyal to their God shall stand firm and take action.*" God will give you courage to stand. Stand before those in authority, in government, on your job, and in your neighborhood. God will give you courage to stand and testify before the city council, before the council commission, or before the school board, and stand up for our children.

In our communities we have to teach our children and promote *brains* over *bling*. We have moved from court-ordered desegregation to integration, but most of our children still do not perform to their full capacity. We must encourage them to stand for what is right. Further, we must give them the tools to succeed and to survive. The Holy Ghost will stand for you in situations when your back is against the wall.

The Holy Spirit stood inside our ancestors: Sojourner Truth, Harriett Tubman, Jarena Lee, Frederick Douglass, and Martin Luther King Jr. In our spirit, we must determine and confess with our mouth, ""I need God to get inside my life and fill me with Holy Ghost Power!" Yes, if you look at the situation in your flesh, *fear* will try to overwhelm you. "I'm scared." "I'm nervous." "I don't know if I can handle . . . ." "Everybody is against me." "I can't do this." Fear starts to rise.

When danger surrounds us, instead of being filled with faith, we'll find ourselves paralyzed with fear. We need to be reminded every now and then that God responds to faith. Fear says one thing. Faith says another. But the Spirit of God wants to give you victory. God wants you to go forward. God wants us to remember: "Greater is *he* that is in me that he that is in the world. When fear tries to hold you back, we know faith will give you the power to push down walls. Fear says, "My enemies will come against me." Faith says, "Though a host should come against me . . . ." Fear says, "I don't know how it is going to work out . . . ." Faith says, "And we know all things work together for good for those who love God and are called according to his purpose." Fear says, "I don't know where to turn." Faith says, "In the time of trouble he shall hide me." Fear says, "I am worried." Faith says, "Don't worry, if God be for me, . . . " Fear says, "They are attacking me." Faith says, "No weapon formed against me shall prosper."

I am very concerned about young people. Every day, too many are growing up like weeds on a vacant lot and being shot down like animals in the street. We must tell them that the requirements for this new millennium and beyond will be much more than a handshake, or the right haircut or the right clothes. We must get them ready so they will not fear. Often television programs teach our boys how to become barbarians and our girls how to become prostitutes. We must prepare them and tell them that the requirement is to know the English language, both oral and written, which in the past and still too often remains our primary deficiency.

We must tell our youth that life is a hard ball game and the bases are *loaded* against them.

We see what is happening to them through the camera lens. They are *loaded* with those who would take away affirmative action gains, ignore our civil rights, acknowledge reverse discrimination, reduce scholarships, grants, and aid money for students. They are *loaded* with those who would tell our young people to be carefree, adventuresome, and exploratory instead of telling them to be qualified, competent, informed, and excellent.

And so the call goes forth for Christians who have a story to tell. It goes forth for those who are ready, willing, and able to stand on the front line with courage and determination. It goes forth for those who look to the hills from which comes our help, knowing our help comes from the Lord. It goes forth for those who are ready to move; ready to take on the challenges of the day and not be afraid.

We need *soldiers* of *bold faith.* Men and women who believe the word of God, which says, "I can do all things through Christ who strengthens me." We must be brave, daring, and bold when we are asked, "Who is on God's side?" realizing we may sometimes stumble but we refuse to fall. We may bend but we refuse to break. We may get tired but we refuse to quit. We may be burdened but we are not bound. We are soldiers, Christians of bold faith, ready to reclaim our communities and our streets, Christians who are ready to reclaim our children, Christians who are ready to say yes to the Lord and no to the world, Christians who are *ready to tell their story to a dying world that Jesus lives, because he lives on the inside; for there is a war going on.* But the

God would have us to know "greater is he that is in us than he that is in the world." God wants us to know there is nothing the devil can put against you that God cannot conquer. There is nothing Satan can do that God cannot undo. There is nothing Satan can undo, God cannot put together again. *There is a war going on,* and God has the great battle plan and an exit strategy.

When the attack of the adversary comes against you, God always has a plan. We cannot figure it out. We cannot categorize it, or reorder it, or reorganize it. We cannot analyze it. There is no paradigm for it.

But we trust God and know God is still in charge of the universe. And when God gets ready, God is going to send God's son to receive us as God's own. When Jesus comes, he is looking for a church without a spot or a wrinkle. When Jesus comes, he is not going to look for a Baptist Church, Methodist Church, Pentecostal Church, Presbyterian Church, Episcopalian Church, Adventist Church, or Nondenominational church. Jesus is going to look for a church without a spot or a wrinkle. Not a building, but people who have been "steadfast, unmovable, always abounding in the work of the Lord."

Will you be ready when he comes? Do you want to be good soldiers? No matter how hard it is now? No matter how difficult it may seem? No matter how dark it has been? Just know one day Jesus is coming back. John said in the book of Revelation, "Lo, I looked and there was a number that no man could number. And they came from all over the universe." They came from California, Maryland, Alabama, Pennsylvania, New York, New Guinea, Ghana, Somalia, Liberia, Nigeria, Germany, New Orleans, and New Zealand. And they had on their long white robes.

And the Bible says they began to march and to march and to march! *Soldiers* in the army of the Lord. One of the angels touched another angel and said, "Who are these?" and the angel said, "Oh you know who they are. *These are they* who have come up out of great tribulation. *These are they* who had a story to tell. *These are they* who lost their jobs and could not pay their bills. *These are they* who had sickness in their body. *These are they* who could not afford to be sick and did not have medical insurance. *These are they* whose friends turned their backs on them. *These are they* who were talked about and persecuted. *These are they* who have come out of great tribulation and their robes had been washed in the blood of the Lamb. But the Bible would have us to know that Jesus will wipe every tear from our eyes. We know not the day nor the hour, but as *soldiers,* we must be ready when he comes. I want to see Jesus. I want to be in that number.

By our deeds and declarations, let us be known. One day Jesus is coming back. He will step out into the midst of the ethereal sky and we will be caught up to meet him in the air. It will be a grand reunion indeed. It will be the small and the towering, the old and the young, the black and the white, the rich and the poor. It will be all of us.

Those who have been faithful, up on high, Jesus will call by our name and make rulers over many. So we come knowing we have a story to tell. Therefore, *when asked the question "Who died and gave you a story?"* you can say with confidence, God said, "*I am* whatever you need me to be. *I am* the one who can pay your bills when there is no money in the bank. *I am* the one who can get your husband off crack and bring your children back home. *I am* the one who will make your enemies stumble and fall. *I am* the one who can grant you that promotion when they keep overlooking you. *I am* the one who can make your new business flourish. *I am* the one who can provide all your needs according to my riches in glory. *I am* the only one who can forgive your sins and give you everlasting life."

What's your story? Are you a child of the King? God will never leave you and me, never forsake you and me, never mislead you and me, never forget you and me, never overlook you and me, and never cancel our appointment in his appointment book! God is God. God is faithful. We are God's, and God is ours.

My Father in heaven can whip the father of this world, and so, if you're wondering why I feel so secure, understand this: God keeps God's promises. God said it. I believe it, and that settles it. I agree with the songwriter William Ogden who wrote in 1887, "We have a message from the Lord, Hallelujah! A message, my dear friend, for you. It's recorded in his word, Hallelujah! Jesus said it and I know it's true. Look and live, my brother, live. Look to Jesus now and live. It's recorded in his word, Hallelujah!

It's only if you "look and live." Amen.

CHAPTER 11

PUSH PAST YOUR PAIN

Corliss D. Heath

Read: 1 Samuel 1:11–18

When I became serious about losing weight, I took up spinning or what some call indoor cycling. I went to spin class at least twice a week and grew to love it so much that I invested in cycling shoes and other gear. Spinning was a stress reliever for me, a way to unwind after a hard day's work. However, spinning or cycling is not something that one should jump into impetuously. You have to mentally and physically prepare for the class because getting through can sometimes be a challenge.

There were days when the instructor showed no mercy. When sensing, however, we were at a point of stopping or giving up, she often told us to PUSH! There were times in class when we felt we'd reached the edge of our body's limits and wanted to take a break, slow down, or just plain quit. But during those moments she encouraged us to keep going and to press on beyond the feeling of wanting to stop, because doing so builds endurance, muscle, and strength, as well as character. We were told to exercise at our own pace and not to compete with others because everyone was at different stages in their cycling. No one, however, regardless of his or her spinning experience, wanted to be viewed as the person who couldn't hang with the class. There were days when my legs burned, but I kept cycling. There were days when my knees hurt, but I kept cycling. There were also days I thought my instructor was possessed because of the workout she gave us. But in spite of how I felt, I was committed to losing weight as well as committed to the class. Therefore, I kept cycling and pushed past my pain.

Webster defines pain, in part as a localized physical suffering associated with bodily disorder; acute mental or emotional distress or suffering, grief. Accordingly, PAIN represents *P*ersonal *A*nguish *I*nvoking *N*ew levels, new heights, or new dimensions.

The book of 1 Samuel introduces us to a time when ancient Israel is on the brink of radical transformation. This is a time situated between Judges and Kings when the end of an unstructured and unstable tribal mode of life is soon to culminate, and a centralized political system of institutionalized monarchy is on the horizon.

Yet, in the midst of all the social, political, and economic happenings of Israel, we are introduced to a woman named Hannah and hear the story of her longing to experience motherhood—better yet, a story depicting her pain. Although she is not often talked about, Hannah contributes very significantly to the life of Israel's history. Hannah was one of four women in the Old Testament who dealt with the issue of barrenness. The others were Sarah, Rachel, and Rebekah. Hannah was considered the most prayerful of the four women.

Hannah was an Ephramite and was married to Elkanah, who also had another wife named Peninnah. While the Bible states that Hannah was Elkanah's favorite of the two women, the fact still remains that she was barren. Like many of us, Hannah was very much aware of all that was happening in the world around her, all that was going on in her town, as well as in her community. But she was so consumed with her own issues and her own pain that she ignored or muted out everything else going on. After all, she was barren, which to her was the same as saying she had no hope for a future.

As a result of her barrenness, Hannah became bitter. She also battled with depression and despair, due to the ridicule of Peninnah, her husband's other wife. Peninnah, to Hannah's dismay, gave birth to several children, perhaps as many as five or six. Hannah felt hopeless, powerless, and, some may even say, she felt stuck. Her emotional and mental state affected her appetite. She was not eating and, I can imagine, she probably was not sleeping well either. Being barren affected the way Hannah interacted with her family and no doubt her friends—especially if they had children. And to make matters worse, Hannah's husband could not understand why she felt the way she did.

Elkanah could not comprehend why it was so important for Hannah to not only bear a child, but to bear a son (to carry on the family name). Hence, this made Hannah all the more frustrated.

When we stop to think about it, Hannah had a lot to deal with. She couldn't have children; her husband didn't understand her situation or her feelings; not to mention, the other wife was taunting her and giving her grief. If the truth be told, many of us can identify with Hannah. We are so consumed with life's circumstances that we don't know what to do. Whether it's when the phone rings, when we go to the mailbox, or when we check e-mail, it seems like it's always something going on. We encounter situations we never dreamed of and wonder when or if our circumstances will ever change. At the same time, some of us identify with Hannah because we are in a state of barrenness and have become resentful as a result of our inability to produce. Regardless, however, of what we are going through, we must know that God is able to speak in the midst of a barren situation. In fact, time and time again throughout the Bible, we find where barrenness becomes the arena of God's life-giving action. Likewise, Hannah's story teaches us how to push past the suffering and pain we sometimes must endure in life.

The first thing we learn about pushing past our pain is that Hannah knew where her strength lay. Hannah was at her wit's end. She was frustrated, fed up, and tired of living in a barren state. Yet we find that her frustration worked as a positive for her because it empowered her. It empowered her to a point of radical prayer and worship. We already know Hannah was a praying woman. However, the text shows us that the frustration of her pain pushed her to a new level of prayer. The Bible tells us she prayed in such a manner that Eli, the temple priest, thought she was drunk. Thus, Hannah's praying was not viewed as unusual, but the way she prayed in order to move past her pain was indeed extraordinary. Being at a point of desperation, Hannah's prayer was not seen as just an ordinary religious practice, but instead it represented an act of faith, strength, and power.

Major change can take place when we become so frustrated with our present situation that we refuse to remain in the state we are in. Rather than settling for failure or disappointment, we sometimes have to step back and ask ourselves, "What options do I have?" or "What options have I not considered?" It takes strength to push through a painful situation and strength to work at bringing about change. Strength is built in part by stretching ourselves, taking consistent action, and meeting personal expectations that prepare us for the next level. Also, like some of us in spin class, strength lies in the ability to reach down within and connect to our inner power source when we get weak, slow down, reach our body's limit, or are on the verge of giving up.

Another thing we need to know about pushing past our pain is that we must stay focused. Things may not look good right now. Likewise, it may appear as if nothing is changing. But we must stay focused and remember, God honors faithfulness. Although Hannah was not happy in her present situation, she never took her eyes off God. She didn't give up on her goal of having a son. No matter how hard it was for her to see the other mothers, to endure the ridicule of Peninnah, she never turned her back on God. She never stopped praying. She never stopped going to church. I can only imagine her sometimes questioning God, asking, "Why me?" or "How long?" Yet through all of her hurt, pain, and disappointment, she still remained focused.

When things aren't going our way, we often have a tendency to run away from God, instead of running to God. Sometimes we stop praying. We stop going to church. Likewise some of us throw up our hands and stop everything, all together. As if we were doing God a favor in the first place. However, even in times of crisis, we must remember what we were called to do and walk in our purpose, no matter what the situation looks like, despite the turmoil and anguish that may be going on in our lives. Regardless of how people may treat you or try to keep you from reaching your goal, look beyond all that is going on around you and keep your eyes on God.

Finally, change may not come immediately, but we can REST in the assurance that God will take care of us. God will fix our situation and give us the desires of our heart. In the midst of everything going on around Hannah and inside of her, God never allowed the madness and confusion to overtake her, not through pain and tears, not in times when it seemed like some didn't understand and others just didn't care. Not in times when we feel like giving up, but something inside keeps telling us to hold on a little while longer. Like Hannah, it's during those times of struggle that we can find comfort and refuge in God.

In 2010, I went back to school full-time to work on my PhD. My decision to quit my "good government job" as my dad would say, to go back to school full-time was similar to my decision to take up spinning. It was not something I did impetuously. Needless to say, the journey to obtaining a PhD has not been easy. But amidst my losses, disappointments, hurts, setbacks, and, yes, pain, God has sustained me. I don't always understand why some things happen the way they do, but nevertheless, I know God has my best interest in mind. People don't always understand my methodology. Some even question my decisions, and it's not always easy to explain. But the gospel group Mary Mary says it best in their song "Can't Give Up Now": "I just can't give up now. I've come too far from where I've started from. Nobody told me that the road would be easy. But I don't believe God brought me this far to leave me."

Thus, a key element to my being able to rest in God is having a personal relationship with God. Through relationship, one learns that progress comes as a result of process. Likewise, having a relationship with God helps us to understand what Mercy Odeyoye means when she says, "*I came to regard my suffering as birth pangs, having the faith that something good will come out of all that I go through.*"

Despite what you may be going through now, know that God is both willing and able to open up your future. God wants to birth some things in each of us. However, it is important to know that conception and delivery both have their appointed times. When Hannah finally gave birth to Samuel, she gave him back to God. Although she wanted a son to honor her husband, she realized her being able to have a child wasn't really about her. It was about what God wanted to do through her. Such is the same with my obtaining a PhD. Through this process, I have learned that it is not about me or the degree itself, but what God will have me to do with the knowledge obtained with the degree. Therefore, I share a little of what I have been through with the hopes it will encourage and enable someone who feels like giving up to continue to press his or her way through and push past the pain.

God has the ability to change your circumstances. But are you willing to do what it takes to bring about the change? In order to reach your goal, to walk in purpose, and to live out your destiny, you must be able to tap into your inner strength and stay focused. Moreover, you have to make up your mind that no matter what the situation looks like, how you feel, or what ridicule you may endure, you will keep pedaling and push past your pain.

CHAPTER 12

FOR REAL, FOR REAL

Angelique Mason

Read: Revelation 22:1–7

The term, "For real, for real," is commonly used by young people when they are trying to stress a fact. In January 2011, God blessed me with a job working with women in crisis. The one thing all the women have in common is a warped sense of reality. They come either to receive help because they are homeless or about to be homeless. How many of you know that homelessness is defined as anyone over twenty-one years of age who does not have a lease with his or her name on it? *For real, for real,* some of our children living in our homes would be defined as homeless.

The women may be eligible to receive either permanent housing or transitional housing depending upon their circumstances but "John Jones" cannot come and live with them. *For real, for real,* some of them will jeopardize a roof over their heads for a man in their beds. This is their reality.

Working for this organization made me realize that our society does not have a keen sense of reality. That is why so many of us tune in to reality shows on a daily basis. We try to cover our pain and suffering, our trials and tribulations, and our passions by watching other people struggle. We watch them being demoralized, bullied, and humiliated to the point of tears because it makes us feel better about our own situations.

For real, for real, reality television is television programming that presents allegedly unscripted dramatic or humorous situations, documents actual events, and usually features ordinary people instead of professional actors. Sometimes they are featured in a contest or other situation where a prize is awarded. This type of programming has existed in some form or another since the early years of television. Reality television began as a television formula in the 1990s and exploded as a global phenomenon around 1999–2000.

Reality television frequently portrays a modified and highly influenced form of reality by utilizing *sensationalism* to attract viewers and to generate advertising profits. Participants are often placed in exotic locations or abnormal situations. Sometimes they are coached to act in specific *scripted* ways by off-screen "story editors" or "segment producers" with the portrayal of events and *speech* manipulated and contrived to create an *illusion* of reality through editing and other post-productions techniques.

For real, for real! Hollywood writers and their union have a little secret they want to share: Some of the reality shows that are dominating the prime-time airwaves are—spoiler alert!—not really real! Meaning, the writers say that the shows are written. They have scripts, called "paper cuts" in the trade. Jokes are penned for hosts and banter for judges. Plot points and narrative arcs are developed. And, in some cases, lines are fed directly to the contestants. (*The writers do not claim that the voting is rigged.*) For real.

Not by accident, the scribes say, the reality stories have a beginning, middle, and end that is shaped by writers who are not called writers but "story editors" or "segment producers." These individuals use the art of switching around contestant sound bites that were recorded at different times and patching them together to create what appears to be a seamless narrative. The reality programs are, undeniably, a new kind of hybrid entertainment. The Writers' Guild is not claiming that the shows are faked, but it insists that—*for real for real*—a lot more typing and manipulation is employed on them than many viewers might guess.

Reality television works because it is relatively cheap to make. Prime-time reality is a nice little business. The problem is—writers on reality are not really writing in the traditional sense. There is no script. What they are doing is shaping the shows, which is different.

For instance:

Survivor. Survivor is a *reality television game show* format that is produced in many countries throughout the world. The show maroons a group of strangers (as one or more tribes) in a desolate locale, where they must provide food, water, fire, and shelter for themselves while competing in challenges to earn either a reward or immunity from expulsion from the game in a successive set of elimination votes. Sometimes medical conditions, such as injury or infection, have eliminated several contestants. *For real, for real*, someone needs to tell them that *God will meet all your needs according to the riches of his glory in Christ Jesus.*

During the course of the game, players compete as tribes or individually in contests called challenges. Challenges consist of *endurance*, strength, agility, *problem solving, teamwork, dexterity*, and/ or *willpower*, and are usually designed to fit the theme of the current season. A common style of challenge is a race through a series of obstacles to collect puzzle pieces, which must then be assembled after all the pieces have been collected. The last two or three survivors face a jury composed of the previous seven, eight, or nine players voted off. That jury interrogates the final few and then votes for the winner of the game, the title of Sole Survivor, and a million dollar prize. *Judge not lest ye be judged.*

Big Fat Loser is another reality show. Kai Hibbard, a former contestant on "*The Biggest Loser*," has decided to come forward and shed some light on how such major pounds are really shed on the show. Wait—reality TV isn't real? *For real?* Props to Kai for coming forward to admit that she participated in a myth that hurts people.

A week is not really a week on TV. For real, for real, those twelve-pound weight losses you see happen in more than seven days. Good to know. Weight Watchers would die if someone lost twelve pounds in a week.

The weight loss methods weren't always healthy. Because big weight loss numbers draw big ratings for the show, there was pressure from producers to crank up the volume. *For real*, Kai left knowing how to "dehydrate" before weigh-ins. "Dehydration" is a method of temporary weight loss where people can exercise excessively, wear warm clothing or garbage bags, use a sauna, chew gum, or use diuretics to lose water weight before a weigh-in.

Contestants were encouraged to engage in unhealthy eating practices. Kai says she left the show with an eating disorder. The pressure to perform left her with a warped body image and an unhealthy relationship to food. The show considered coffee an acceptable meal supplement. *For real, for real,* her hair fell out. She had extreme anxiety, and her family and her husband had to stage an intervention.

The Biggest Loser contestants are under hush-hush contracts, which are fairly standard practice for reality TV. Kai's reality is that she may get sued for sharing these stories.

The Bachelor is a reality series that gives one bachelor the opportunity to meet the woman of his dreams. The bachelor is introduced to twenty-five women at a cocktail party. At the end of the evening, he selects fifteen women from that group by giving them a single red rose. At this point, and at every point thereafter, the women can either accept or decline the bachelor's invitation to continue. The women who accept the rose move into a mansion overlooking the Pacific Ocean for much of their courtship with the bachelor. Via a series of dates and social gatherings, the number of romantic hopefuls narrows from fifteen to eight, then four and, ultimately, to one woman who captures his heart. But, if he pops the question, will she accept? Men, correct me if I'm wrong, do you really care if she accepts your proposal? *For real, for real,* you can sing the jingle, *"I've had the time of my life."*

Now, one of my favorite shows is *The Amazing Race. The Amazing Race* is a reality television game show in which teams of two people, who have some form of a preexisting personal relationship, race around the world in competition with other teams. Contestants strive to arrive first at *"pit stops"* at the end of each leg of the race to win prizes and to avoid coming in last—which carries the possibility of elimination or a significant disadvantage in the following leg (segment). Contestants travel to and within multiple countries in a variety of transportation modes, including *planes, balloons, helicopters, trucks, bicycles, taxicabs, rental cars, Jitneys, trains, buses, boats,* and *by foot.* The clues (cryptic hints) provided in each leg lead the teams to the next destination or direct them to perform a task, either together or by a single member. The challenges are related to the country wherein they are located or its culture. Teams are progressively eliminated until three are left. At that point, the team that arrives first in the final leg is awarded a grand prize.

The stress of racing with one's partner, staying ahead of the competition, completing the assigned tasks, and dealing with little sleep or luxury combine to create "killer fatigue," a phrase coined by fans of the show, and often a team's inability to cope with the fatigue is what is ultimately responsible for a team's elimination from *The Amazing Race.*

For real, for real, "and let us run with perseverance the race marked out for us, fixing our eyes on Jesus, the pioneer and perfecter of faith. For the joy set before him, he endured the cross, scorning its shame, and sat down at the right hand of the throne of God. Consider him who endured such opposition from sinners, so that you will not grow weary and lose heart.

My favorite reality show is *Undercover Boss.* The episode will follow an executive as he or she examines the inner workings of the person's company by working alongside employees to learn the effects their decisions have on others. These executives find where the problems are in the organization and see some of the unsung heroes in low-level positions.

"Everyone has daydreamed about watching the boss do his or her job," said CBS Entertainment president Nina Tassler. "The journey of watching a chief executive walk a mile in employees' shoes is always very revealing, often humorous, and, in some cases, very inspiring."

John 1:14 says, "The word became flesh and made his dwelling among us. We have seen his glory, the glory of the one and only Son, who came from the Father, full of grace and truth."

Now, I want you to journey with me to the book of Revelation. John is the writer of this reality show. John, the disciple that Jesus loved. John, the man who was given custody of Jesus' mother from the cross.

Tradition says that John remained in Jerusalem until the death of Mary, which occurred around the middle of the first century. Then he moved to Ephesus, where he probably wrote the Gospel of John and the epistles of 1 John, 2 John, and 3 John.

Now, God did not inspire John to write the book of Revelation to the seven churches to satisfy their curiosity or to inform them about the future. At the time, Christians were being persecuted under the reign of Domitian, Roman emperor from 81 through 96 CE. The worship of the emperor was being rigidly enforced because Domitian claimed divinity and wrote a decree that once every year all Roman citizens and slaves had to bow down before an image of him and revere him as lord and god.

For real, for real, God said we should not bow down to or serve any images, for God is a jealous God, visiting the iniquity of the fathers upon the children to the third and fourth generation of those who hate him, and showing steadfast love to thousands of those who love God and keep God's commandments.

Later in John's life, he was banished by Domitian to the island of Patmos. There John was forced to work in the mines, where the Romans hoped he would die from exposure to the elements. How many of you believe that what the devil means for evil, God will use for the good?

While on the isle of Patmos, around the year 95, John had a unique reality experience. This was *his first vision*. He wrote that on the Lord's day, he heard a loud voice telling him to write on a scroll and send it to the seven churches in the province of Asia. John is the human author who simply wrote as the Holy Spirit inspired him. He prophetically commented on the churches according to what he was told.

In John's *second vision*, two great things are seen. First the throne of God is seen, and God, God's self, is holding a book, a book that contains the destiny of the world in the end times. However, the book is sealed and no one is found to be worthy to open it. Just when John feels a sense of despair, the Lamb of God, the Lord Jesus Christ, steps forward. The Book of Destiny is opened and the trio of judgments is revealed:

- the seven seal judgments: God's wrath

- the seven trumpet judgments: these will be unleashed upon the earth and

- a third of the population will be killed, but the good news is that a remnant will be saved

- the seven bowls of wrath:

1st bowl—Similar to the sixth plague on Egypt, the entire population of the world suffers from incurable infections (boils and sores, HIV/AIDS, hepatitis B and C)

2nd bowl—One third of sea life had been killed during the sounding of the second trumpet, but now all sea life is killed.

3rd bowl—The earth's fresh water becomes polluted—could this be the reason for the oil spills: Exxon/Alaska, BP/Gulf of Mexico, and radiation/Japan?

4th bowl—The sun's heat intensifies, causing dramatic changes in the atmosphere and climate—this could explain global warming. We can only tell what season it is by the budding of the trees.

5th bowl—This will have grave psychological effects—manic depression, bipolar disorder, and schizophrenia. Could that explain shootings at Columbine High School in Colorado, at the military base in Fort Hood, Texas, and at the grocery store in Tuscan, Arizona?

6th bowl—The great river, Euphrates, will dry up to prepare the way for the kings from the *east*. This could be the economy. Who are we borrowing money from? China. Isn't China in the east?

7th bowl—A series of natural earthquakes, more devastating than ever before experienced in history, will take place. These disasters include massive earthquakes proven to dislodge islands, level mountains, and destroy cities. Louisiana, Indonesia, Haiti, and Japan have experienced disasters. The state of Maryland has even experienced some tremors in the past.

The angel said to me, "These words are trustworthy and true. The Lord, the God who inspires the prophets, sent his angel to show his servants the things that must soon take place."

John hears a "loud voice speaking from the throne of God announcing the advent of God." God will dwell with humans as a community. God will comfort all anguish, and death, pain, and grief will be no more. Now God speaks directly to John. Prior to this, it was angels. God tells John to write:

- God is the cause and conclusion of all things. God freely offers the gift of the water of life. God also pledges to be God and father to those who overcome.

- John sees a river coming from the throne of God; and the tree of life bears different fruit every month, and its leaves have healing properties.

• This city is a place for the worship of God and the Lamb. There is nothing cursed there.

For real, for real, I got some good news. In John's final vision, he says he sees that the first heaven and the first earth has passed away to make room for a new heaven and a new earth. John writes he sees the Holy City, the New Jerusalem, and he describes the New Jerusalem as "a bride beautifully dressed for her husband." Jesus is inviting all who thirst to come and drink from the water of life at no cost.

Did you get your invitation? If not, let me share what I received: *"The Spirit and the Bride together with the Father invite you to share in their joy as they are joined as one on this first day of Eternity Future in the Throne Room. Supper following!*

This is not the time to watch the reality game shows like "Let's Make a Deal." If you want to play games, play "The Price Is Right" and "Be in It to Win It." You are probably saying to yourself, *For real?* I say to you, *For real!*

CHAPTER 13

BUILT FOR THE ROAD AHEAD!

Carolyn Ann Knight

Read: Isaiah 43:1–7 NLT

I have discovered, the older I get and the longer I live, that I am no longer a big fan of television. It may seem strange to admit that in an age of cable, digital, satellite, and high-definition television; in an age of big screen, wide screen, and screen-in-screen television, I cannot find much on the small screen that captures and holds my attention. However, at the same time, I have discovered I am a big lover of television commercials. I am fascinated by the advertising industry's thirty- to ninety-second assault upon my fashion, financial, fun, and food habits. I love exploring the creative genius of marketing executives as they attempt to tap into the spending, buying, and consuming habits of the average American. I love commercials. I love commercials with children and animals in them. I love commercials with cartoon characters. I love commercials with music. I love commercials that make me laugh. I just love commercials.

My favorite commercials of late are car commercials. I like to see cars racing around corners, talking to other cars, sitting on the streets begging their owners to take them for a drive, cars playing ball, or cars displayed on the showroom floor. The more I watched car commercials and got into car commercials, I noticed there is a similar pattern to all car commercials. Each car commercial will usually display the car with its many features and then close the commercial with a tag. The tag is a memorable line car sellers want you to remember. It is the hook that they hope will make you choose their car over all the other competing models. It is the one thing they want to stick in your head when you are looking for a brand new car. You may be familiar with some of these tags: Mazda: "Zoom! Zoom!" Volkswagen: Drivers wanted! Hyundai: "Drive your way!" Chrysler: "Inspiration comes standard!" Cadillac: "Breakthrough!" Buick: "Dream on . . . Dream until your dreams come true!" Lexus: The passionate pursuit of perfection! BMW: "The ultimate driving machine." Hummer: "Like nothing else!" I noticed that Mercedes-Benz and Jaguar do not really have tags. I guess they believe the name speaks for itself. However, my favorite tag of all, and the one I use for this sermon, is from Ford. Ford says their cars are: "Built for the road ahead!" I have borrowed Ford's tagline for the title of this sermon: "Built for the Road Ahead!"

I like that. The Ford Motor Company believes they have designed an automobile that can handle the road, any road that is out there. Whatever the circumstance, the situation, or the condition, Ford claims they have built a car that can handle it: the expected and the unexpected, the planned and the unplanned, the wanted and the unwanted, the seen and the unseen. Ford says, bring it on. In making such a claim, Ford is saying that what we put in our cars—the material we use and the aerodynamic configuration of our models— are engineered in such a way as to take the pressure off today's driving conditions. Further, in making such a claim, Ford is saying they expect their cars to be driven, that is, they want their cars to go somewhere, anywhere. But more than that, Ford executives believe that no matter where their cars are driven—on dirt roads, on two-lane streets, on four-lane highways—they expect their cars to be able to perform on the journey and they expect their cars to handle anything that might occur on the journey.

In this context, I want to suggest God is making the same claim about each and every one of us that Ford makes about their cars. We are "built for the road ahead." As we consider the task before us as women of God, women of faith and service, we are uniquely created, shaped, and designed to handle anything we will face in this life and in ministry. That is, from head to toe, front to back, through and through, we have everything we need to make it in life and in the ministry.

When the people of Israel found themselves transitioning from one place to another, from one people to another, from one paradigm to another, they were reminded in the closing verses of chapter 42 of just how difficult their journey had been. In chapter 43 of 2 Isaiah, the children of Israel hear the salvation oracle from God. God had promised to be with them in an unusual alliance as they moved forward into their future. This text is a word of promise and assurance for all of us who are about to move into God's planned future for us. Look again at what the text says: "They are not to be afraid for God has ransomed them." God, the creator of everything that is, has intervened on behalf of this exilic people to claim them and deliver them. God had called them by name, and God has identified them as God's own and entered into a nonnegotiable agreement to be with them in every possible circumstance.

When they go through deep waters and great trouble, God will be there. When they go through rivers of difficulty, God will be their lifeguard. When they walk through the fire of oppression, they will not be singed, scorched, nor will they smell like smoke. Why? Because God is with them. God has promised to help them maneuver the rough terrain of the journey ahead of them. The Exodus is behind them. The Red Sea experience is behind them. Now they are moving into a new relationship and a new future with God and the world. As God declared to God's people in the first chapter of Joshua, they are not to be afraid, for God is with them. They have God's identity upon them. Not only has God redeemed them, but God has identified them as God's own. They belong to God.

God has a unique and abiding relationship with these persons who, although not perfect, are special to God. Now they are ready to move in faith and become the people God created them and designed them to be. And as we move through the various seasons of life, many of us have our own individual and collective stories to tell about life and living. Each of us is filled with the cumulative emotions of our own exilic condition whether we came from Atlanta, Albuquerque, or Alabama; whether we moved from Minnesota, Marietta, or Memphis; or if we came by train, bus, or plane. We all have a story to tell about the exilic experiences of life and living. There are some experiences behind us. There are some things we are facing right now. There are some things we all must face in the future. But, thank God, we made it this far.

Therefore, in this text we find a word of challenge for where we are today. Not only as women in this world, not only as African American women living in a hostile world, and not only as African American Christian women in church and community with all of its many challenges, changes, and crisis. This text finds us as women of faith, courage, and conviction moving methodically through this menacing third millennium.

Many of us will live our lives as productive capable citizens and leaders doing work and ministry well into the twenty-first century. We need to have a course of action that will make the church better, make the community stronger, and make the culture richer. All of us should have a goal for our life and our ministry that we are going to fight for what is right, stand for the truth, defend the poor and the oppressed, succeed in everything we do, and make a name for ourselves. Let me suggest this to all of us as we celebrate milestones. It is a great time to be alive. We celebrate our history at one of the greatest moments in human history. We savor the great work that has been done by great and noble women down through the years. We, as women, will do what we have always done. We will go out into the real madness of this world and make a difference. We face a real world with real people who have real problems and real pain. There are women and men who stand in need of what we have.

Make no mistake about it, there is a new world and a new church out there. It is a postmodern church. It is a postmodern world. It is a church in the world and a world in the church. It is a high-tech, multimedia, global world/church. It is the world/church of the iPad, iPod, MP3, Android, Blackberry, videophone, and digital camera. It is a church that is multicultural, multiracial, and multigenerational. It better be the church of personal piety and prophetic witness. It is the church of holy hip-hop and the holy roller. It is no longer the church of the big hat and funeral home fans. It is no longer the church of one husband, one wife, and 2.5 children. It is the church of the praise team and the hymnbook. It is the church of the prayer meeting and the support group. It is the church with men and women in ministry. It is the church of not only black and white worshiping together, but also gay and straight worshiping together. It is the church of the shout and the silence. It is the local, rural, community, and mega church working together to save souls, defeat Satan, and do justice.

We now live in a world where terrorists are daily trying to take over, where 911 is so much more than an emergency phone number. We live in a nation that is bruised and battered by indecisive leadership, arrogance on Wall Street, anger on Main Street, fear on every street, a filibustering Senate, a confused and chaotic Congress, unsafe courts, bullet-ridden streets, gang-infested schools, and unhappy homes, four protracted wars, high unemployment, and inadequate health care. We live in a world where levees break and expose the issues of poverty and race in this nation. We live in a world where we are more obsessed with rich, spoiled, talentless young people on their way to jail and rehab than we are with young men and women coming home from Iraq and Afghanistan in body bags.

I want to remind us of the words of this text: "When you go through deep waters and great trouble, God will be with you. When you go through rivers of difficulty, you will not drown! When you walk through the fire of oppression, you will not be burned up; the flames will not consume you."

As we move methodically into this third millennium, we need to be reminded that it will take the corporate, collective, and communal strength of each and every one of us to become all that God intends for us to become. We need to be reminded to do all that God has assigned us to do. Moving forward in this world, we need the old and the new. It is not the young folks nor the old folks alone who can move us forward into our destiny, change the world, teach our children, fight every battle, or build God's church. Rather it is the young folks and the old folks working together that will get the job done.

As we move forward, we need the young folks and the old folks, linked together, working together to get things done. What we need today and in the future is the wisdom of the seasoned saints and the energy of the youth. What we need is the maturity of the aged and the flexibility of the young. What we need is the stability of one generation and the possibility of the next generation. Those who are young should spend time with older adults. Get to know them and learn from them. Those who are older should mentor and encourage young people at every available chance.

All that we have experienced in the world, in our life, and in the church has been designed to get us ready to face life and ministry in the twenty-first century. The mercies of God have been with us. We, as sisters, have weathered the storms of history, honored our great and noble past, and made our mark on this world. All that we have been through so far was getting us ready for the road ahead. Every situation that you had to deal with in this church and in your personal experience is but a microcosm of the real world ahead. Every up and every down, every trial, every triumph, every victory, every defeat, every joy, and every sorrow has been getting us ready for the road ahead.

This is why the text uses the word "when," because struggle in ministry and life is inevitable. All the translations I read and studied for this passage use the word "when." They did not use "if" but "when." Doing so suggested to me the inevitability of hard times, rough places, and difficult situations in life and ministry. *When* you come, not *if* you come to a hard place. *When* you face, not *if* you face a tremendous challenge in ministry. *When* it gets too hard for you, not *if* it gets too hard for you. God will be with you. As we gather as sisters to pull together, strive together, work together, we are built for the "road ahead." That is why we must have a better attitude, a better outlook, and a clearer perspective about our faith and our future. We must remember we are stronger together, better together, greater together than we are separately. We can do more, serve more, give more, and go further than we ever thought, hoped, or dared to dream. Whatever we are going to do in the future will take our shared humanity working toward our common interests, common causes, and common circumstances. God has already given us everything we need to reach that destiny where every child can learn, every senior will be safe, and every person will be able to take her or his place in this world. We are blessed to be a blessing.

We are ready to move out, move on, move up in life, in ministry, and in this world. We are ready to make our mark, make our contribution, and make a name ourselves. Everything we have experienced and are experiencing is getting us ready for the road ahead. Nietzsche, the nineteenth-century agnostic philosopher, said, "If it doesn't kill you, it will only make you stronger! It will make you better!"

I love the Ford commercial. I like it so much that I made it my personal theme for life and ministry. Every morning when I wake up, I tell myself I am "built for the road ahead!" At night, after I say my prayers I say: "Thank you, Lord; I am built for the road ahead." But there is something about that commercial I initially found troubling.

I had a question for Ford that nagged me and I needed to find the answer. I wanted to know how Ford knows their cars are "built for the road ahead." They do not know what is ahead. They have not driven their cars on every road, in every town, in every state. How then can they make such an august, somewhat arrogant, audacious claim? I kept watching the commercial and the commercial never answered my question.

I went to the Ford website and the website helped me out. The website had information about the design of the car. The website shared how the car is actually made. In other words, even before the car is a car, it is designed to handle the road ahead. They do not wait until the car is finished and then declare that it can handle wind, rain, snow, and ice. Before the car gets to the drawing board, before it hits the assembly line, before it comes to the factory, it is designed to handle tough conditions. When it is in the designer's mind, it is getting ready to handle the road ahead. Before we got here, before we said yes, before we even heard the call or answered the call . . . or knew anything about a call . . . God was getting us ready to handle the road ahead.

But wait one minute! Have you ever been up late at night watching TV because you were unable to sleep? If you have, then you have discovered that the commercial has a cousin. It is known as the infomercial. The infomercial is longer than the commercial in that it gives you all of the specific details of the products being sold. As the infomercial goes on, just when you think the announcer has told you all you need to know about the product, the announcer says: "But wait—there is more!"

I kept reading the material on the Ford website and discovered that not only are Ford cars designed to handle the road ahead, but before every car, truck, or van leaves the factory, it is put through a rigorous road test. The road test is a simulated driving scenario that tests the car's ability to handle actual driving conditions. They drive the vehicle through rain, wind, snow, and ice. They drive through potholes, around curves, and up mountains to see if their cars can handle these conditions. What are you trying to tell us, Carolyn? I am so glad you asked! Whenever you go through anything in life or in your ministry, think of it as a road test. Everything you have experienced in your life, think of it as a road test. In every problem, think road test. In every pain, think road test. When you remember every mean professor or person, think road test. Whenever you think of every unpaid bill, think road test. Whenever you remember every missed meal, think road test. Whenever you remember every lonely night, think road test. Whenever you remember every difficult assignment, think road test. Whenever you think about every disappointment, think road test. Whenever you think of every unkind word said to you, think road test. Whenever you think of every boring class, think road test. Whenever you think about every closed door, think road test.

But wait—there is more! Not only does Ford put their cars through a rigorous road test. Every now and then they are required to perform a crash test. Periodically, Ford will take a car, truck, or van and crash it into the wall at speeds of up to one hundred miles per hour to see how much damage it can take. The difference between the road test and the crash test is that they use real drivers in the road test. In the crash test, they use human-like models. In the road test, they bring in trained drivers, close the roads, and warn persons like you and me not to try their experiment at home. In other words, they want you and me to know that even though their cars can stand up to any condition, they are intended to be driven on normal roads, at normal speeds, and under normal conditions. But they also want you to know when their cars meet the abnormal conditions of driving as they sometimes will, they can handle it.

However, when they do a crash test they know that no matter how skilled the driver, somebody can get hurt. So in the crash test they do not use a trained driver, they use a human-like prototype. They use a model in the shape of a human being who can handle the crash. Now this is the shouting point in this sermon.

You have done the road test. So far, you have passed the road test. But you do not have to take the crash test. I know somebody who took the crash test so we would not have to. I know somebody who took the crash test so we could handle the road test. Jesus Christ did the crash test so we can handle the road ahead! And now we are ready to move forward together to make the world and the church, our families and our homes, our schools and our businesses better. Jesus did the crash test so we can handle the road ahead.

CHAPTER 14

A LOVE THAT KEEPS ON GIVING AND FORGIVING

Frances "Toni" Murphy Draper

Read: Luke 7:36–50

When I was eight years old, my family moved to Baltimore from Washington, DC, into our very first house. It wasn't a very big house, but it had a nice backyard. Often, the neighborhood girls came into the yard to pick daisies, which they assured me would confirm a boy's affection. "He loves me, he loves me not," we chanted as we plucked off each petal. If you said, "He loves me," when you pulled the last petal, you were convinced you had found true love. But if you plucked the last petal on the words "He loves me not," well, you just picked another flower hoping to get a different outcome. Even if you managed to finally get a "He loves me," most eight-year-old boys could care less—unless you also could hit a baseball or run a touchdown. If by chance, you did become boyfriend or girlfriend (whatever that meant), it rarely lasted more than a couple of weeks!

I'm glad God's love is not so unpredictable. God's love is not something you find "on a two-way street and lose on a lonely highway." you don't have to ask God, "Will you still love me tomorrow?" or "Where did your love go?" God's love is so amazing that it keeps on giving and forgiving.

The Bible is filled with examples of God's love from Genesis to Revelation, from Adam and Eve, to the prodigal son, from the rebellious Israelites to the lukewarm Laodiceans, from the woman at the well to the thief on the cross to the ultimate sacrifice, Jesus Christ himself!

A great example of this love is found in our text: Luke 7 beginning with verse 36. Jesus is invited to dinner by Simon, the Pharisee. Pharisees were religious folk—preachers known for establishing their own righteousness, folk who trusted in themselves, who leaned on their degrees and pedigrees, their works and their own interpretation of the law.

In verse 30 of Luke 7, we're told that these Pharisees rejected the will of God, rejected God's plan for them, and rejected God's purpose for their lives.

But even though Simon, the Pharisee, had turned his back on God's plan for his life, Jesus still went to his house for a banquet. Why? Because Jesus wanted to prove a point about love.

In those days, banquets were public affairs. You couldn't eat without an invitation, but you could come in and observe the proceedings.

So, according to verse 37, a woman—a known sinner, probably a prostitute—heard that Jesus was at Simon's house—Jesus, the healer; Jesus, the miracle worker; Jesus who had a rep for loving even the most unlovable. This woman didn't go to Simon's home because she deserved to be there, but because she was convinced that Jesus loved her in spite of all she had done and all she had been through. All she wanted to do was to love Jesus back.

Yes, she was a sinner, an outcast. In fact, Simon couldn't believe she had the nerve to show up at his house. Yet, when she heard Jesus was there, she came—just as she was—for the sole purpose of loving on Jesus, of worshiping him with her best.

She was like the woman with the issue of blood—she pressed her way, in spite of her past, in spite of the gossip, in spite of what she wore, in spite of where she lived, in spite of how much money she had, in spite of the hurts caused by people in her church, in spite of her failures, her faults, her disappointments, her depression, and her distress.

She didn't come because she liked listening to the choir, she didn't come because Simon lived in a magnificent mansion, she didn't come to be seen or to hook up with the brother she saw going into Simon's house, she came to worship the King of Kings and the Lord of Lords. She came to worship Jesus. How do we know?

Unlike Simon, she does everything for Jesus. She washes Jesus' feet, not with water, but with her tears, and dries them with her hair. She then humbles herself by bending down and kissing his feet and anointing them with expensive perfume. She could have let her past derail her purpose. She could have kept beating herself up over things that happened years ago (or maybe they happened last night). She could have hid out and acted like she didn't know Jesus. But she understood that God loved her so much that God was willing to give God's only son Jesus to die on a cross for her sins, and she was grateful!

On the surface, Simon had much more than this woman. He was a preacher/teacher. He had a title. He was used to people waiting on him hand and foot. He had a nice house and a fancy "BMW" chariot; he was somebody's somebody. He was on the OWN network and the Word channel, and had a closet full of designer tunics, but he didn't understand that without Jesus, his righteousness was as filthy as rags.

The woman who anointed Jesus is aware of her sin. Her many tears indicate she knows how far she has come because of the love of Jesus. She washes, kisses, and perfumes Jesus' feet with an attitude of gratitude. She loves much because she has been forgiven much. And she is much forgiven because God is love! All she can do now is bow down in Jesus' presence.

Simon, on the other hand, is so self-righteous that he doesn't even recognize he's in need of a savior. After all, Simon knows the letter of the law. He's gone to the temple religiously. He knows all of the dos and don'ts. Simon, however, misses it. It's not about the law, the "thou shall nots," but about God's love.

Beloved, God is love. Jesus loved this woman unconditionally, and because of this he was the focus of her heart. It's like the love my grandmother, Vashti Turley Murphy, had for her five daughters. She often wrote long letters to them—like the one she wrote to her oldest daughter, on March 11, 1936:

> Dear Bettye,
> This morning nineteen years ago God gave you to me. Despite the ups and downs and the differences of opinion, if I could have the choice of a million dollars or you, I would take you—even if they baited me and said we will give you all the gold in the world. Darling, what memories each of your birthdays I recall. I wanted you so much. For months, I joyfully awaited your arrival. You are certainly the culmination of my dreams.

Beloved, Jesus loves you and he loves me the same way. His love is not based on your past but on his purposes for your life. Jesus' unconditional, undeniable, unquestionable love never runs out. It's a love that keeps on giving and forgiving.

So pick up your flowers, and begin plucking the petals . . . Ready? He loves me. He suffered for me. He loves me. He bled for me. He loves me. He died for me. He loves me. He rose for me. He loves me. He's coming back for me. He loves me. He loves me. He loves me. And because Jesus loves you, you should love the Lord your God with all your heart and with all your soul and with all your strength and with all your mind. Love your neighbor as you love yourself.

You can't make Jesus stop loving you. When you mess up, Jesus loves you; when you go astray, Jesus comes after you; when you try to hide out, Jesus finds you; when you miss the mark, Jesus forgives you. All Jesus wants is your love in return. May the ever-giving love of God sustain you, encourage you, engulf you, redeem you, refresh you, and renew you.

CHAPTER 15

IN SPIRIT AND IN TRUTH:
There's Only One Way to Do This!

Carolyn D. Showell

Read: John 4:23–24

At any given moment, any chosen individual can accomplish a task, produce an idea, or arrange an encounter that those who experience it will declare was God-inspired or inspirited. Sometimes these encounters are the result of an exceptional gift, an unexplainable presence, or perhaps an unusual ability. There is this sense of "awe" and "wonderment." These are the times when it is clear that "divine thought" or the "holy intelligence" of God has found a "useable" vessel in the earth—a person who is aligned with the purpose of God and who stands in agreement with God's will.

We must understand that the original intent, plan, and knowledge of God is to constantly seek and search for a person, place, situation, or arena in which it can "enter" into "time" and make God recognized, known, and revealed. Our God who dwells in eternity does indeed also live and operate in time. And so it is with us—the dualism of our spiritual existence causes us to live concurrently in time and eternity. Right where you sit trapped "in these fleeting moments," you also sit "beyond these finite moments." And, at any given time, that which is eternal will thrust itself into time to become visible and manifested through anybody and anything that is paying attention to God. These "intrusions" or "interruptions" cause minutes to take on a significance that is more than a "normal" or regular occurrence.

In Jewish thought, it is called, "sanctified time." These are moments in time that have been set apart for intentional concentration on God. While we are yet bound by time, we make time holy by making it about God and what is important to God. Thus, we are not guilty of "killing" or "wasting" time by being engulfed in activities that do not glorify God. These moments become different from other moments of the day when we bring every thought, feeling, attitude, and desire into the "presence" of God. It is there, in God's presence, that our thinking is refreshed and transformed.

This must become our expanded understanding of the nature of our "worship" and why we *must* worship in these latter days. Our coming together can no longer be "just" a real good, feel good time. It cannot be a time of pretense or performance. Because of the times in which we live, we must take every opportunity to gain new intelligence from the Spirit of God.

Worship must become a time when the true worshiper will reach beyond the immediacy of the moment and step into the "realm" of the Spirit and experience Truth. It must be an occasion when we enter into God's ultimate reality. The place where God desires to be revealed to us—released in us—to restore for us—and confer upon us. First Corinthians 2:9 declares, "So that we might know that which he has prepared and made ready for us *before* the foundation of the world" . . . in eternity . . . . so that we can know those things which are spiritually comprehended and apprehended!!

Genesis 1:1 teaches us that there is a "causative relationship" between Spirit and speech. Genesis 1:1 says, "In the beginning, God." John 1:1 declares, "In the beginning was the Word." In rabbinic exegesis, it tells us at the beginning of anything that is to be manifested or established by divine blue print, you *must* have God (Spirit) and God's Word (truth). We can, therefore, conclude that, at the beginning of a thing, especially where there is chaos, confusion, and lack of purpose and order, you *must have the presence of God (Spirit)* and God's Word (*truth*).

Truth connected to Spirit becomes a tool of creation. This truth has the power to discover, uncover, and recover that which has been lost in the darkness of chaos and obscurity. Truth becomes a "life giving" language that is the verbal articulation of the Spirit. For this reason, Christ admonishes us in Revelations 2:11 and 17, to hear what the Spirit has to *say* . . .

Oftentimes, mindsets are shaped by previous experience, perceptions, and erroneous misconceptions. Preconceived thought patterns, unmovable strongholds, and bad behavior become a hindrance to spiritual growth and maturity. You must understand that "truth" is the "only" linguistic expression that has the God-ordained ability to challenge, confront, and correct everything that attempts to undermine the "holy intelligence" of God and God's purpose. Truth wrestles with the "lies" within our lives and reconnects us to the authenticity of who we were created to be in God.

It is for these reasons Jesus did not address what is "true," factual, or real within the personal story of the woman at the well. Jesus already knew the issues of her situation. He knew the roots of her behavior, struggles, pain, and abuse. He knew the complexities of her personal reality and how they came to be. But Jesus did not take time to judge or condemn her. Instead, Jesus set it to the side in order to introduce her to a "truth" that would move her life beyond what was "merely true." He introduced her to the "transforming" and "transporting" power of worship. As Jesus stood as the Spirit of Truth, Jesus reconnected her to who she was called to be according to his will. Because in the realm of the Spirit and in the ultimate reality of God, this woman was never called to be a victim of her circumstances, mishandled and misused. "And you shall know the truth and the truth shall set you free." Through the worship of God, she was able to see herself through the eyes of God. Worship allows the true worshiper to reposition her or his spirit, mind, and body into the presence of God's reality, where there is "fullness" and the "completeness" of all things. The "truth" about life is in God's presence. Because it is only in God that we move, live, and have our very existence. The only way to live in accordance to the will of God is that you *must* worship and serve God in Spirit and in truth, because God is looking for those who will worship him like that.

It is in the ultimate reality of God that we are the instruments of God's glory, the re-incarnated word that dwells in the earth realm, an expression of God's thoughts—a reflection of holy intelligence, the tabernacle of God's presence, the latter house of God's power, the seeable—touchable—embodiment of God's greatness. There we walk boldly, live fearlessly, and function with authority. We live in the realm of faith, and favor refuses to let you go! We define and redefine. We give new meaning and significance to the existence of people, places, and things. We live in the overflow of abundance and flow in the spirit of wisdom, knowledge, understanding, and revelation. We live "loved" and "empowered" in Spirit and in truth!!

CHAPTER 16

A MINISTRY OF HEALING

Judy D. Cummings

Read: Mark 1:29–32

After Jesus' triumphal entry into Jerusalem before he is crucified, he spends time with his disciples teaching them and praying for them. Jesus says to his disciples, "Whoever believes in me will do the same works I have done, and even greater works because I am going to be with the Father." This is both a command and a promise!

Yes, we are saved to do the greater works! What are the greater works? Well, Christ Jesus is deliverer, so, we are to deliver. Christ Jesus is healer, so we are to heal. Christ Jesus is the bread of life and the living water, so we are to feed the hungry and quench the thirst of a dry and disillusioned world. Oh, to be more like Christ, that ought to be our desire. And, beloved, that's why it is imperative for us to consider our ministry of healing. Jesus left us a ministry of healing.

Don't you know this ministry we have in these earthen vessels includes the touch of healing? Today, to be an effective body of believers, I submit to you we must become agents of healing. We must be willing to restore and liberate those who are ill and filled with disease back to a healthy relationship with Christ, with their loved ones, and, yes, even with themselves.

Beloved, we are called to make ourselves available to God, to be used as agents of restoration and liberation.

And that's what a healer is, an agent of restoration and liberation. Healers restore those who are in a diseased position back to a correct position. Healers bring holistic care into our lives and healers treat the feverish anguish of our society. You do know our society is burning with a fever, don't you? What an appropriate metaphor. Temperatures are running hot. People are living with anxiety and we are overcome with stress. We have hypertension and hypotension. We are physically overweight and mentality overworked. The truth of the matter is, we are ill. Our fevers are raging. Yes, we are sweating each other to get our voices heard and our needs met.

Lobbyists and politicians are sweating congress with concerns for environmental control, gun control, and birth control. Police and investigators are sweating foreigners for the threat of terrorism and minorities for the threat of guns. We are sweating our government for affordable health care, more social security, unemployment benefits, and safety net measures. We have mothers sweating the fathers of their children for more financial support and contribution of time; children are sweating parents for lessons in adulthood and independence. Our world is sweating with the potentials of nuclear holocaust and genocide. We had pastors sweating whether to vote for Obama or not because of his personal beliefs about homosexuality. We had presidential candidates sweating about health care, the deficit, jobs rates, and Big Bird. Now we have a president sweating a super majority!

Not only that, but church temperatures are also running hot and we are a world running with a fever. And yet the fever is not the cause of our condition! After all, a fever is never the cause but rather the symptom of something else going on deep inside of us. We, as the church of Jesus Christ, cannot afford to just treat the fever, or treat the symptoms! No, no, we must address the root cause of the fever with the courage and conviction of our faith.

Beloved, we cannot afford to live our lives reacting to the symptoms of a larger illness. No, we, the disciples of Christ, are called to be healers! Understand this. True healing addresses the cause, gets to the root of the cause of the disease. The problem, however, is that we are too concerned and too satisfied with just treating the symptoms of an ailing world. The truth is, you cannot fix it until you face it. You cannot heal it if you don't know it needs healing. In my church, we treat the symptoms of homelessness with our feeding ministry, our food pantry, and sponsoring Room in the Inn. We treat the symptoms of drug addiction and prostitution by supporting programs at Renewal House, Magdalene House, and other shelters. We treat the symptoms of teens at risk with our various meaningless activities for young people. We treat disenfranchisement in our communities by giving handouts. Beloved, we are not called to merely apply band-aids to open, hemorrhaging wounds. No, no, we are called to the ministry of healing and liberation. We are called to bring light to dark communities. We are called to heal a world in crises. In order to heal it, we must address the cause, the hegemonic structures, the evil, and not just the symptoms!

If you have been living your life in the shadows, let me enlighten you and share that the root cause of the fever in our world, in our community, and, yes, even in our homes is sin, and the destructive behavior of Satan's kingdom against God's kingdom. You do know we are in warfare. You do know your biggest enemy is not Iran test-firing missiles or those who on September 11th attacked the United States, or those who attacked the consulate in Benghazi, or folk in places like Nashville whose agenda it is to resegregate schools, or folk who want to close hospitals such as Metro General Hospital where the poor and the dispossessed go for health care?

You do know we wrestle not against flesh and blood, but against powers, and principalities, and rulers in high places? We are dealing with Satan and his kingdom of darkness. As healers, it is our task to reclaim the territory Satan has taken from God's kingdom. We have to reclaim our homes, reclaim our children, reclaim our community, reclaim our finances, and reclaim our freedom from the enemy. Christ wants us to reclaim that which is ours.

Look at the text. Peter has decided to leave everything behind, including his family, to follow Jesus. He has listened to Jesus teach, heard him preach, watched him heal and deliver others, yet, in his own home there is a sickness, a fever. Although Peter has a strong relationship with Jesus, when it comes to Peter's home, things are out of control. Many of us are no strangers to that condition. We pray for everybody else. You may see your prayers for others being answered, yet your prayers go unanswered! Things at your house are out of control!

Like Peter, we too live our lives from the inside of a fish bowl. We too have watched others get their breakthrough, watched others achieve their success, watched others get delivered from the same habits and addictions we have, watched others get healed and cured from the same illnesses we have. Sunday after Sunday, we watch Jesus move in the lives of others, wondering when we will get our breakthrough. Lord, when will I get my blessing? Lord, when will salvation come to my home? Lord, when will my mother get off her sickbed? Lord, when will my husband fall on his knees and give his life to Christ? Lord, when will my child begin to behave properly and do well in school? Lord, while you are blessing others, bless me, even me, Lord. Like Job, we've examined our lives. We've been faithful in our giving. We've been faithful in our worship and our service. Yet, in our homes, there is a sickness. Some things are out of control. But there is good news for us this day. The good news is this: Jesus has the cure for what ails. Jesus has a remedy for sickness and the disease within your home. Yes, even in our sick communities and in the world.

In the text, after preaching and teaching, Jesus shows the disciples the sermon is still not done. The final amen has not been said. The expressed faith spoken in worship must now be fulfilled in the home. That which was preached must now be practiced. Peter takes Jesus home. Peter takes the Savior to his home. He didn't leave Jesus at the church but he brought him to his home.

Let me put a pin there! So often, when we leave the church house to go to our own house, to the White House, to our jobs, to speak with our state and local officials, we leave Jesus behind! We leave the sermon we clapped for and nodded in agreement with on the church pew. Some of you go home empty. But the Word from God for us is, in order for salvation to come into our homes, our immediate territories—we need to take Jesus with us. Take Jesus with you. Take him to the place that is broken and shattered. Take him to the place that is chaotic and confusing. Take Jesus with you!

The Bible says Simon Peter's mother-in-law was in bed with a fever. I don't know with which physical illness she had been stricken. As prevalent as breast cancer is among women, she could have had breast cancer. Today, it is a known fact that one in eight women will develop invasive breast cancer over the course of their lifetime. We don't know the nature of the illness of Peter's mother-in-law, but, whatever it was, she was sick. Further, she had not been healed by any other means available to her including Christ's disciples, who had been given the authority to heal, to deliver, and administer the grace of God.

But the good news is, when Peter and the disciples realized the system was broken, they had the good sense to call on the Lord, to take him to the place of brokenness. Jesus went to Peter's house and, when he saw Peter's sick mother-in-law, Jesus wasted no time and immediately administered healing her. Jesus went to the issue. He went to the system, to that which needed to be healed, to that which was holding a child of God captive! Beloved, that's what we must do! We cannot sit back and wait for broken systems, broken people, unfair laws, and unfair practices to come to us. No, no! We are called to be healers and we must go to the place where healing is needed.

The reason many states have administered voter identification laws is because we sat back and did not speak healing to that which was sick, and, like a cancer, it spread. The reason children continue to fall behind, not meeting the standard competencies in school, is because we sit back. There is a reason why breast cancer is not diagnosed in African American women until it is in its later stages. There is a reason why our new super majority chose not to vote for Affordable Health Care—which they like to call Obamacare. Beloved, Jesus did not wait for the sickness to show up on his doorstep; he went to the heart of the matter, and so must we! God has given each of us a ministry of healing. Healing may not be one of your spiritual gifts but all of us have been given a ministry of healing. We must speak truth to power. We must go to that which is sick, that which is broken, that which is in bondage, that which needs a healing touch from the Lord and apply the healing balm of Gilead to that situation.

So let us go forth as the body of Christ, serving as agents of healing in this broken world filled with all manner of sickness and disease. Then, let us lift up Christ by reaching others with a healing touch. Let us reach others with the healing hands he has given us. Look at your hands and say, "These hands are anointed! These hands will break down walls! These hands will open doors! These hands will set the captives free! These hands will clothe the naked! These hands will heal the sick! These hands will raise the dead! These hands will cast out demons! These hands will give God the glory! These hands will give God the praise! These hands will celebrate the goodness of God! These hands will give God adoration! These hands will give God jubilation!"

There is power in our hands. Power to heal this world, power to heal this community, power to heal our neighborhoods! There is power in your hands! Use them to heal for the glory of God. Amen.

CHAPTER 17

HAVE FAITH IN GOD'S PROMISES

Sheila R. McKeithen

Read: Joshua 1:5, Isaiah 43:2, Jeremiah 29:11 NRSV

There are times in our lives when it feels as if we are on a roller coaster ride. Sometimes we are "riding high" and everything is going our way. There are other times when we feel our life has hit a "sudden curve" and we are plunged into the lowest of circumstances. No matter whether or not you believe you are "riding high" or "not riding at all," I want you to remember God is with you. I want you to remember God loves you and will, therefore, never, ever abandon you. In those moments when you feel lonely, I want you to remember that you are not alone. God is with you. God is also with your loved ones. God is with us all and, therefore, we need not be afraid.

I invite you to give up your fear and embrace your faith. I offer you the opportunity to exchange your uncertainty for the certainty that "everything is already alright." If you are willing to live in the faith and certainty that God is in charge of your life, even as you face unfavorable conditions and circumstances, I guarantee you that your faith will "see you through." I did not say your faith will give you exactly what you want. I said, your faith will "see you through" whatever you are going through. Your faith will enable you to stand firm on God's promises even if tough times arise. Faith that looks to God as your strength, deliverer, suppler, healer, comforter, banker, provider, and restorer will see you through every time and without delay.

You ask, "How do I know that this is so?" I know it is so because, like many of you, I, too, have been on that rollercoaster ride. Life has not been an eternal trip on the "up slope" of the rollercoaster of life.

There have been "low moments" for me just as there may have been low moments for you. Even so, we each are and always will be God's children. God's love for us does not and will not change. As we look to God and God's promises to us, we are able to stand on those promises, no matter what is happening around us or to us.

What is a promise? Webster's Dictionary defines promise as "a legally binding declaration that gives the person to whom it is made a right to expect or to claim the performance . . . of a specified act." As a child of God, there are biblical promises we can rely on, for they bind God to perform. These promises also confirm we have a right to expect God to perform that which was promised. If we have faith in God, then we have faith in the promises of God. Let us not abandon our faith in God when the going gets a bit rough. Instead, let us affirm our faith in God and God's promises. Your faith in God breeds confidence in God's promises. Your confidence is directly related to your level of expectation. When your level of expectation is high, you are more likely to comply with that which God requires of you. What are God's promises to us? There are many promises and you can find them in your Bible. Allow me to direct your attention to three of God's promises.

Promise #1: "I will not fail you or forsake you" (Josh. 1:5 NRSV). God is a present help for you at all times. Do you feel like you have failed or fallen short in some way? If so, what is preventing you from getting up and trying again? The answer is "nothing." Do you feel the task before you is too big for you to accomplish? I say to you nothing is too hard for a child of God. In faith, turn to God in prayer. Ask for directions on what you are to do and how to do it. Be willing to surrender the project or task to God, so God's will and not your personal will can be accomplished. Oftentimes, our mind is set on a particular result, in a particular way, and for a particular time. What if the way we have declared is not God's way? What if our timeframe does not coincide with God's timeframe? What if what we want is not what God wants for us? Many times there is a delay in the fulfillment of God's promise because the peephole through which we look is too narrow. The narrowness of our perspective does not allow us to grasp the big picture God wants us to see. The period of "seeming" delay is actually the time for you to mature or grow up out of the narrow confines of your perspective so God can bless us in ways we have yet to imagine.

If you expect to be successful in your endeavors, if you expect God to fulfill the promise, you must confidently perform that which God gives us to accomplish. Do things God's way and in God's time. God assured Moses' successor, Joshua, that if Joshua remained strong and courageous and if he acted in harmony with the laws of God, Joshua's success was assured. God requires no less of us. We must be both strong in our faith and be courageous and bold as we act on God's instructions. We must keep the instructions of God in our heart as we look neither to popular opinion nor to the voice of our own fears. Acting in love with the best of intentions, we reap the fruitage God has promised to us.

Sometimes God's instructions may seem a bit strange. Sometimes, the directions God gives to us make no sense to the human mind. However, if we faithfully and confidently move in obedience on that which God gives us to do, we will reap in due season. The fruitage will be the evidence of God's presence in our lives. Why not try God? Turn to God in prayer and then move into positive action as God directs. In faith and confidence, expect God to fulfill every promise made to you.

Promise #2: "When you pass through the waters, I will be with you; and through the rivers, they shall not overwhelm you; when you walk through fire you shall not be burned, and the flame shall not consume you" (Isa. 43:2 NRSV). News reports of destruction and loss of lives due to floods, fires, hurricanes, and tornado winds are not uncommon these days. Some of us may know people who have lost their home and possessions due to the ever-changing weather patterns. As a pastor, I have stood with families whose homes were flooded and thereafter declared by the government officials to no longer be habitable. These families, many of whom owned their homes, were displaced with no place to live. I have seen firsthand how devastating it can be when the floodwaters recede and families are left to clear away debris, rebuild, and refurnish their home. I have personally swept mud from homes that were flooded. I have helped to physically remove items that once belonged to the sea from the living spaces of friends. These are the realities we face all too often. The right thing to do is to pitch in and do what we can where we can to support adversely impacted families and communities.

Through it all, we must not forget God's promise to be with us even as we begin the process of rebuilding. The God who formed us has promised us that whenever we pass through the waters, God would be there. In fact, if you have had to pass through rough waters, rising rivers, raging fires, and strong winds, your presence is proof God traveled with you. Don't you know it is by God's power and presence that you survived the water, the flood, and the wind? The waters didn't overwhelm you because God is with you, just as God promised. In faith, look back and say what Marvin Sapp sang: "I never would have made it without you." God says, "Don't be afraid. I'm going to show you how to navigate through the water, the fire, and every situation."

What does this mean for us? It means we have to keep our eye of faith on God. We must keep praying. We must keep the promises of God on our lips. We must allow the Holy Spirit to write a message in our heart. We must be tuned into what God is whispering in the silence of our soul. We must obey God's instructions. We must expect God to show up with a workable plan. We must trust that God's plan is always for good and that it will work if we dare to work in harmony with it.

Let us not act as cowards when the rivers rise and the fire burns out of control. Instead, let us be mindful of God's promise that is rooted in God's love for us: "I am with you." When circumstances appear most chaotic, remember: God is with you. Know that you belong to God and that, as a child of God, you are assured there is a way out of every fire, every flood, and every adverse predicament. With our eye looking in faith to God, we will be shown the way through every adverse situation. God's plan for good prevails every time. Let us not judge by appearances. God's will is often hidden below the circumstances of life and not easily perceived by those who lack faith. But the faithful shall see and experience God's salvation again and again.

Promise #3: "For surely I know the plans I have for you, says the LORD, plans for your welfare and not for harm, to give you a future with hope" (Jer. 29:11 NRSV). It is really wonderful to know the God who made you has a plan for your life. God's plan is for good and never for evil. I like to refer to God as the Great Plan Maker. As such, I am reminded to keep turning to God for the plan for my every endeavor. If I follow God's plan, I experience a future with hope.

When I don't follow God's plan, I experience feelings of hopelessness. As always, it is up to every individual to make choices that assure the fulfillment of God's promises. If you find yourself feeling hopeless, dare to believe God has a plan. Turn to God in prayer and simply say: "God, I'm listening for the plan. I need to hear from you." Then, get still and listen for God's instructions. When you go to sleep, ensure that there is a writing pad and pen near your bedside. God's plan may be revealed to you as you sleep, or even as you wash the dishes. The point is this: Once you ask God for the plan, you must stay awake, alert, and aware for that plan. Be prepared to capture it when it is revealed in your soul.

If you are experiencing feelings of distress over a situation, turn to God for the plan before you move into action. Too often we turn to God only after our personal plan fails to produce the desired results. In faith, let us allow God to lead us in this journey called life. Consult God's wisdom *before* you act. In all situations, know that your trust in God's presence, your faith in God's promises, and your dependence on God's plan will forever see you through.

Let's pray: "Dearest Lord, I turn to you for a full understanding of your plan for my life and for this situation. I surrender my will, so that your will may come forth. I stand on your promises that they may be fulfilled here and now. In faith, I release the past and open myself to the glorious future you have ordained for me. For every blessing that is even now raining upon my life and this situation, I give thanks and simply say, Amen."

CHAPTER 18

WHEN WOMEN HAVE WINGS

Jessica Kendell Ingram

Read: Revelation 12

In my reading of the word of God, I came across this text and it captured my full attention. I wanted to gain an understanding of the implications of these words, as I was especially intrigued by its reference to women having wings.

Because I am seminary trained and I do believe in doing my exegetical work, I visited the commentaries. I read what that had to say, but none of them spoke to my spirit. None of them were moving me in the direction God wanted me to go. And so I beg you to forgive me, those of you who have trafficked in the halls of academia. Forgive me for not properly exegeting this text and giving you all of the background about the writer, why he was writing this text, the cultural context, where he was when he wrote it, what the imagery meant, the symbols, the interpretations, etc, etc. Please allow me to share what God has given to me just for you.

This is what God dropped in my spirit to share with you. Whenever we as women are on the verge of experiencing a new dimension in God, whenever we have decided to really walk with God, when we have accepted our kingdom assignment and are willing to make the sacrifices and complete our work, when we have received the vision and worked without ceasing to bring it to pass, when we have seen our future and it looks better than our present reality and so we keep on doing the will of God even though we are going through hell in our present reality, when we are on the verge of receiving the long-awaited promises of God, when the manifestation of what God said God was going to do for us is just about to happen, when our midnight is getting ready to turn into a bright sunny day, when God is getting ready to turn our situation all the way around, when we are about to give birth to our dreams, when our waiting is almost over and, any day now, the manifestation of what we have been waiting for is just about to happen—this is when the enemy will come after us with all of his power, with all of his imps, with all of his might and try to utterly destroy us. And the enemy will do it by any means necessary. Do I have just one witness?

And if you are not careful, if you do not understand this spiritual phenomenon—that although the devil is not characterized by the "omnis"—that is, he is not omnipresent, he is not omniscience, it is not omnipotent, he is not everywhere, he is not all knowing and he is not all powerful—I can tell you he does know when God is getting ready to bless you beyond measure and so he will do whatever he can to make you give up, lose your mind, go into a deep depression, cry all the time about the least little thing. Somebody may look at you wrong and you feel like crying, you get a run in your stocking and you just break down, the dog chewed up your good shoes and you become hysterical.

The tactics of the devil will cause you to doubt God, to question God, and to not believe God. The devil will make you feel like "what is the use?"—what's the use of all of this praying, all of this fasting, all of this reading the Bible, all of this sacrificing, all of this hard work on my job, in my church, in this ministry?

You may ask: What's the use of me giving all of this money, paying my tithes and offerings? What is the point in me being at church all the time, not just on Sunday morning but at other times during the week? What's the point in me being involved in all of the Women's Day stuff? And I am still going through all of this hell? What's the point in me doing all of this only to have to still deal with a bunch of problems, still find myself facing troubles on every side, still wake up to heartache and pain every day, and still have to deal with crazy folk everywhere I go—right in my house? They have lost their minds. They are crazy as they can be, crazy as a Betsy bug. They are certified, bona fide, and card-carrying crazy!!

Even in the church, some people act like they are on assignment from Satan himself! And now you mean to tell me, I am getting ready to experience some more attacks from the enemy? Somebody has got to help me understand this thing.

Well, I am sharing this sermon to help a sistah out. Now I told you, I did my exegetical work, but it didn't take me where I wanted to go. Instead of the commentators dealing with the writer using the imagery of a woman giving birth, they wanted to talk about some cultural myths of the day and who the woman represented in the mythological stories. The commentary writers did not, in any way, get plugged into a woman's reality. Although the writer who penned the text chose to talk about a woman, the glaring focus of the text, however, was ignored.

Well, I got a download from heaven. The Holy Ghost told me that in chapter 12 of the book of Revelation, the writer John begins to talk about a woman in labor. John talks about her getting ready to give birth to a new reality. While she was on the verge of giving birth, a war broke out in heaven, and a great fiery dragon with seven heads, ten horns, and seven diamonds on his head took his tail and threw a third of the stars of heaven towards earth. Just as the woman was ready to give birth, the dragon stood before her to devour her—to destroy what was getting ready to come forth from her. The Holy Ghost showed me that the writer was referring not just to some cultural myths, but he was speaking about the struggles that real women go through when they are about to give birth to what God has planted in their spirit womb. This scripture passage is really talking about women.

Women are the ones who know about giving birth. Women are the ones who know about the pain of going through labor. Women are the ones who know about carrying a child for nine months while going through morning sickness, changes in the shapes of our bodies, something of which men do not know. Women are the ones who eat strange things, and get all moody. Women are the ones—not the brothers, so I know John was talking to women. Even if you have never experienced a natural birth, you know about giving birth in the realm of the spirit. Women carry visions and dreams, and their kingdom assignments differ from men's.

Women process it differently. As soon as men get the assignment, they want to make it happen right away. Women know it takes time. Therefore, we learn how to wait, how to nourish it, how to feed it, and how to carry it. Yes we do. John was talking to women.

The text shows, not only does the enemy try to destroy what is in us while it is in us, the enemy also tries to destroy it once it is birthed. The text shares that the devil came when the woman was getting ready to give birth. In verse 7, we see that after she gave birth, a war broke out in heaven. So this lets me know we must always be on our spiritual guard when we are carrying the promises of God, especially when they are manifested in our lives. The devil is always on the prowl trying to destroy us. Thus, we have to be spiritually wise woman. Don't be naïve. Don't be unaware. Don't be spiritually ignorant, and don't get caught off guard. You must understand the words of the song, "Nearer My God to Thee" when it says, "my soul be on thy guard. Ten thousand foes arise." You must understand that the devil hates you. He wants to wipe you out!!

Thus, the greater the vision, the dream, the plan, the project, the assignment, the promises of God, or the ministry God has placed in you, the greater the attacks of the enemy.

The woman gave birth to a male child who was going to change the course of history. This was not just an ordinary son. The Bible says he was caught up to God and God's throne as soon as he was born. So the devil did everything he possibly could to the newborn. Therefore, when the enemy knows something great is about to be birthed in you, the enemy will work hard to destroy it. This does not apply only to our dreams, visions, assignments, etc. It also applies to our children.

Let me share something personal. I used to wonder why my only child had so many difficulties. From the time she was a little child, she would get into trouble. In kindergarten, the teacher would send notes home saying she talked too much. Every school she attended, there was some issue. I asked God, "What is this all about?" When my daughter was ten years old, Rev. Jackie McCullough, who used to preach my annual women's revival, met her. Rev. Jackie immediately prophesied to me and my daughter. She said that because of the unusual anointing on my daughter's life, the enemy was trying to totally destroy her. This prophesy has been confirmed over and over again. When my daughter was born, like the child of the woman in the text, the anointing was already there and the enemy came after her immediately. But you must know that the enemy is stupid. The enemy forgot that she had a praying mama who ain't scared. Let me move on, as I could stay right here for the rest of the sermon!

Understand, the level of your attacks is commensurate to the level of what God is doing in you and is getting ready to do in you. So while you are going through trials and tribulations, while you are experiencing the fiery darts of the enemy, you ought to start thanking God!

Another writer in the New Testament said there were many adversaries as a great and effective door had opened for him. Thus, if there is a great assignment on your life, you will experience great attacks from the enemy. If you are working to manifest what God has told you to do, then you are going to go through the never-ending onslaught of the enemy.

I have learned through personal experience that great opportunities equal great opposition. Great anointing equals great attacks. Great visions equal great viciousness from the enemy. Great dreams equal great demons. Great assignments equal great assaults!

Let me get a little personal and tell you this. God once deposited a great assignment in the spirit of my husband, Bishop Gregory Ingram, and in my spirit. God told us to become leaders in our church. Since July 2000, we have experienced unthinkable onslaughts of the enemy to the extent that we began to question if we really heard God's voice telling Gregory G. M. Ingram to aspire for the Episcopacy.

Since we were experiencing so many problems, we thought we should not have moved, and should have stayed in Oak Grove. We would have made major money and should have built a new church by now—even a mega church. We would have built a new home by now. We have been the most powerful clergy couple in Detroit had we not gone through all of the attacks of the devil on our child, on our marriage, on our image, on our character, on our work in the district, on the bishop's body, on our finances, and on the troubles with our family members. I could go on and on, but I promise, we have come to understand that because God has given us a great assignment and we are determined to complete it, no matter what the cost, no matter what we have to go through, no matter the sacrifices we have to make, the enemy wants to stop us! But I tell you, the devil is a liar!

We have come to understand we are not in this by ourselves, and neither are you. While there is a war going on in our lives, in your life in the earth realm, verse 7 of chapter 12 of this book of Revelation lets us know there is also a war going on in heaven. It says a war broke out in heaven, Michael and his angels fought the dragon, and the dragon and his angels fought. But the dragon did not prevail. The dragon was cast out. That old serpent that is known as the evil one and Satan—the one who deceives the world—was cast to the earth and his angels were cast out with him. Verse 12 says he went down to the earth. Satan came down with great wrath because Satan knows he has a short time. Verse 13 says, when the dragon saw that he had been cast to the earth, he persecuted the women who gave birth to the male child.

Please understand that the enemy has come down to the earthly realm to destroy you. When you said yes to God's will and yes to God way, a war broke out in heaven. Satan wanted to stop you. Satan wanted to destroy you. This is why you are going through so much hell. Ole slue-footed Satan has picked up his pace because he knows he doesn't have much time. This is the year of manifestation of all that God said he would do in your life. This is the year when the promises shall be manifested. The blessings shall be manifested. The vision shall be manifested. This is the year!

So, this is why one bad thing after another continues to happen in your life. As soon as you win one battle, another battle comes. As soon as you get through this trouble, another trouble comes. As soon as you can clearly see your way through confusion, more confusion comes. As soon as you have one thing in order, disorder comes. As soon as you make ends meet, another financial challenge comes. As soon as your body is healed, another sickness comes. The wrath of the enemy shifts to the highest level because Satan knows he has a short time.

But wait a minute—in verse 14 there is a divine "but." When you see the word "but," you know God is getting ready to bust a move. God is getting ready to intervene. God is getting ready to reverse some stuff. God is getting ready to manifest God's power.

The text says, "But the woman was given the two wings of the great eagle, so that she could fly from the serpent into the wilderness, to her place where she is nourished for a time and times and half a time."

In the midst of all she was going through with the devil, God gave her two wings of an eagle. Now you must know something about eagle wings—especially female eagle wings. The body length of a male eagle is 30 to 34 inches and the wingspan ranging from 72 to 85 inches. On the other hand, the body length of a female eagle is between 35 and

37 inches with a wingspan ranging from 79 to 90 inches.

The eagle wings are long and broad, making them effective for soaring. Eagle wings allow them to fly up to 10,000 feet, achieving a speed of 30–5 miles per hour. The text said the woman was given the wings of an eagle. Therefore, she was given the ability to fly high, to soar, to go above her circumstance, to fly above what she was going through. She could fly so high that the enemy couldn't reach her. She could fly so high that she could lift herself above ground attacks. She could fly so high that the enemy couldn't locate her on his radar screen.

I just want you to know that when women have wings, the enemy can't harm us. When women have wings, no weapon formed against us can prosper. When women have wings, we can do whatever God has told us to do. When women have wings, our destiny is secure and our visions and dreams will come to past. When women have wings, the manifestation of God's promises will take place in our lives.

Are you a woman with wings? Do you believe you can fly? Do you know that because you have wings, you have the victory? I used to think I could not go on and life was nothing but an awful song. But now, I know the meaning of true love. We can lean on God's everlasting arms. If we can see it, then we can do it. If we just believe it, there's nothing to it. I believe God will enable us to fly. I believe God will allow us to touch heaven. I was on the verge of breaking down. Sometimes, the silence can seem so loud, but there are miracles in life we all must achieve. We must first, however, know it starts inside of us. Oh, I believe God will enable us to fly.

Often we avoid reading the book of Revelation. We avoid it because of our inability to sort through the imagery in the chapters and apply them to our lives. But I have found the book of Revelation to be one that gives profound insight into the circumstances of life. It assures me that, no matter what I go through, I already have the victory. I have also found in this book that there are spiritual nuggets that speak directly to women. Such is the case in this text. I believe the words found in chapter 12 are words of assurances, words that let us know there is a God who understands what we go through, words that instruct us on how to get through rough seasons in our lives, words that gives us strength not just to get through our problems but to enable us to declare victory.

Further, this chapter helps us to declare that while we are in the midst of the worst times in our lives, we can still lift our hands and lavish God with praise. We can praise God because we already know we will come out on the other side wiser, stronger, and better.

So God instructed me to share this sermon so you will believe you are a fierce woman of God—a godly woman who will not allow any demon to back her into a corner. You are a godly woman who will not allow any contrary spirit to make you sit in a place of depression. You are a godly woman who will not allow any attack to cause you to doubt yourself. You are a godly woman who will not allow any adversity to make you an emotional wreck, making you incapable of sound thinking and making sound decisions. You will be victorious!! Amen!

CHAPTER 19

LET A NEW WOMAN ARISE

Vashti-Jasmine McKenzie Saint-Jean

Read: Mark 5:25–34

We have all been tasked to do things that we did not want to: eating foods that we did not like, caring for dogs that had to be walked, preparing for tests and exams that had to be taken, consuming medicine that did not taste good, going to the doctor for medical exams when we did not feel good, participating in conversations we would rather avoid, wearing clothes our parents used to make us wear, and going places we had to go, but did not feel like going.

We have all experienced things we wish we hadn't: the ending of friendships, saying good-bye to lovers and others who just went away, and saying good-bye to others we sent away; taking jobs we didn't like to pay the bills, dealing with changes that were forced upon us, and handling drama we did not deserve. We have had to deal with a hand that was dealt to us whether by happenstance or consequence of an action.

We have done things out of obligation, things in which we felt a sense of duty. The truth is, it is hard to do the things we really just don't want do because we have been beaten down, worn out, taken through hoops, exhausted from the rejection, the trial and error, the disappointments, the delays, and the setbacks of life. As soon as you recover from one thing, immediately you are facing another.

We meet an unnamed woman in Mark chapter 5, described simply by what she was facing at the moment—her issue of blood. Imagine the exasperation of the unnamed woman who had already been to every doctor in town, lost everything she had trying to be cured, frustrated with the fact that not only was she not cured but she was broke, and her condition had gotten worse. And yet, she still pushed towards one last chance at being cured and journeyed toward Jesus. Imagine the mental preparation she had to put herself through as she had to deal with what people would say to her and how people would treat her. People would turn their noses up at her if they were to see this unclean woman walking towards them. She had nothing but hope to lean on as she pressed her way that day.

This woman, whom Marks speaks of, is one who was in need of a supernatural change to the course of her life. This life or the lack thereof, consisted of twelve years where she was secluded in her residence except for the times where she ventured through the naysayers and physicians who declared that her situation was beyond repair. She was excommunicated socially and was living a life of isolation. Her physical condition stagnated every aspect of her life. Her physical condition paralyzed the things around her to the point that her life was at a stand-still for twelve years. We learn from this scripture, without knowing any other details of her life, that this woman had been living in a frustratingly strange season in her life.

Without revealing any other details of this woman's life, scripture tells us she has been living in a frustrating season. Who this woman was is unknown. Her situation and life was overshadowed by her condition and it had made her just about invisible to the society in which she lived. It is a difficult season when the content of who you are, and the context where you find yourself, need supernatural adjusting at the same time.

The content of who you are—your personal life is nonexistent, confusing, or in disarray—and the things that make you who you are, even the very essence of your being, is a distant memory. There is an uncertainty of behavior—a behavior that makes you feel like you are living within a continuous cycle. You need to consider your own issues now (not the children's, the boss's, your sisters' or friends') and at the same time, your context has gone crazy. The woman—you—the very person who sometimes gets lost in the pages of life, find yourself being listed as "the certain and unnamed" woman. And sometimes you get to a point where you are so lost in dealing with the condition, you find yourself lost in existence.

The context—the environment you find yourself in—is out of

whack. Upheaval and confusion seem to be the author of everything that surrounds you. You solve one thing, and just when you think you will get a little relief, something else happens. You can't figure out which way is up because life keeps tossing you to and fro'. Imagine how long the woman with the issue of blood wanted either stability or at least some peace just to be able to accept what God had allowed. Every day she sought an answer and every day she did not receive one, and yet the issue, the circumstance, the condition was still ever present.

On that day, the woman with the issue of blood was still dealing with a conflict with her content and her context. Her issue had isolated her. There was no life to be had. She spent her money on trying to get well. That's all her life was and, although the text does not fill us in, I am sure that's not how her life was before she had to deal with this issue. Her content was nonexistent and her context was nonexistent.

Faced with a situation that hadn't changed in more than twelve years, she did not let the previous failures for a cure stop her, but rather they propelled her to the place where she could seek the healer. She could have given up prior to that day and accepted her fate. But rather, she had a relentless desire to be healed. So she kept trying things that perhaps would work until one day she heard about a man named Jesus. Despite all of what she had been through, she pressed her way to see Jesus. She pressed her way through the crowds that surrounded Jesus and did all she could do until she found herself, knees in the dirt, reaching between the feet of persons who could have easily trampled her. Yet, she reached out in faith and grabbed the hem of Jesus' garment. When she came in contact with the garment, because of her faith, immediately her bleeding stopped.

What can we learn from this woman who took this journey towards Jesus to find healing and restoration? She came to a location where she expected to find Jesus and was met with a large crowd of people. Probably, she couldn't see Jesus but knew he was there. She could not get a break from her issues before then but, on that day, she broke through the crowds to receive her breakthrough. She reached out for the divine with her last hope, the thoughts of last resort with nothing further to lose. The miracle is not only in her healing but that she reached out in faith.

That is what we can learn from the woman with the issue of blood.

Despite our situations, hard times, and setbacks, when we have tried everything but fail over and over again—we can just show up in faith, reach out in faith, and hold on in faith. This is the very miracle that can change our lives. Despite all of our issues, we continue to press our way to Jesus with hope that everything will be okay.

With one touch, Jesus changed her content, and with that her context changed. On that day, the result of her journey to touch Jesus is this: first, the power is not in pressing your way through the crowds, the power is in the journey where you find that God is faithful. The woman had to believe that there had to be more for her life in order for her to even leave her home on that day. She had to believe in the promise that Jesus was a healer.

When both your content and your context need attention—reach for God, not people. Look to God and not the situation that may be overwhelming you. Let a new woman arise! Grab your confidence and go! Retrieve a new sense of self, and press your way to Jesus. Rediscover your nerve. Pull on your faith and watch God change your situation. Let a new woman arise!

CHAPTER 20

THE FIERCE URGENCY OF NOW

Gina Stewart

Read: Luke 13:10–17

July 4th, 1776, was the day the colonies decided to declare themselves independent of Britain. By writing a very detailed decree, they decided they no longer would need to be governed by the rulers of England who had been so very unjust to the colonists in the years before. So on July 4th, America was born.

What is ironic is that, one hundred years prior to America declaring and claiming its independence from Great Britain, in the seventeenth century, Africans were brought to American shores as slaves. They were not freed until President Abraham Lincoln signed the Emancipation Proclamation in 1863. Although the Emancipation Proclamation freed the slaves, Jim Crow laws were created to deny African Americans the benefits of their full emancipation.

It's a strange irony to me. It is strange because it makes me wonder how one group would seek to liberate itself from oppression while at the same time holding another group hostage to the same principle from which they sought to be liberated and freed. Have you ever wondered about that? Have you ever wondered how and why the oppressed oppress others? How do the oppressed out-oppress the oppressor? Why do *some* blacks who have been marginalized, disenfranchised, and oppressed oppress women and children? Why do women who have been oppressed, looked over, locked out, left out, tolerated rather than celebrated, turn around and oppress other women? Why do those who were once outsiders, who become insiders, turn around and oppress the outsider when they become insiders? Why do older members oppress new members and then when new members become old members, the new old members turn around and oppress the newer members? Why do older folks oppress younger folks? Why do we make rules that we break and then turnaround and demand that others follow rules we openly break? It is this kind of hypocrisy and inconsistency that Jesus addresses in the scripture passage.

The scripture passage is a story about a delivered woman. Jesus has just set her free from an infirmity that had her bound for eighteen years. Because of her physical condition, the text does not say anything is wrong with her mind, but for eighteen years because of her physical condition, this woman has been excluded from the privileges of humanity. She is already marginalized because of her gender; however, her condition also contributed to her marginalization.

Luke, the physician, describes her as a woman with a spirit of infirmity—she was a woman with a spirit of weakness or impotence, or you might even say powerlessness. In this instance, Satan stands behind the affliction of this woman.

She had been crippled for eighteen years and was not in a position to lift herself up. The text says she had been bound for eighteen years because of the devil. For eighteen years, she had been staring at the floor; for eighteen years, she couldn't look out of the window; for eighteen years, she was unable to stand, sit, or even lie down in bed. For eighteen years, she couldn't straighten her crooked back. This unidentified woman had been in bondage to an infirmity/weakness that had crippled her and kept her in a state of impotence and powerlessness—for eighteen years.

The text provides no specifics about the root medical cause of this woman's stooped posture—a crooked spine, osteoporosis, arthritis, etc. The text doesn't tell us, but we can be sure she suffered from chronic unrelenting pain. I can imagine that the pain must have been debilitating, limiting, and stressful. And, definitely, a cure or healing for her condition would be liberating.

After she suffered a debilitating illness for eighteen years, something needs to be said for her commitment to attend worship. If I had been crippled for eighteen years, I wonder if I would be faithful to worship God. Longevity in suffering has a way of testing the depth of our faith and our commitment.

Most of us can handle short-term disappointments, sickness, setbacks, interruptions, and abandonment, but long-term disappointments, sicknesses, setbacks, interruptions, and abandonment have a way of testing the depth of our commitment and resilience. It's not as difficult to maintain a consistent level of commitment and loyalty to God when things are flowing according to schedule, but long-term disappointment and disorientation have a way of testing the depth of our commitment. There is something to be said for this woman who is found in worship after suffering for eighteen years.

The text doesn't say it, but I have a sneaky suspicion that this is not the first time this woman has looked for divine help. I have a suspicion that this woman had probably prayed and asked God for help, but was not delivered.

Ah, but it was on this particular day that heaven came to the synagogue. For it was on this particular day that Jesus was teaching in the synagogue on the Sabbath. God incarnate, the word made flesh, truth personified. *Jesus of Nazareth* was teaching in the synagogue. This was the Jesus who had compassion for people; the Jesus who commoners heard with gladness. This was the Jesus who was willing to risk his reputation and social contamination by holding a conversation with a woman at the well in broad daylight. This was the Jesus who forgave a woman caught in the very act of adultery. This was the Jesus who defended the woman with the alabaster jar and said, leave her alone! It was Jesus of Nazareth (who with radar sensitivity and compassion) saw this dejected, disabled, diminished, demoralized, disenfranchised, debilitated, and downcast woman. It was on this particular day in the synagogue that Jesus called her forward to address her.

Jesus initiates the healing. He "summons" her and speaks life to her situation and says, "Woman, be loosed from your sickness," and put his hands on her. When she couldn't act for herself, Jesus took the initiative, broke her isolation, and brought her back into community. Jesus sees her, he speaks to her, and he lays hands on her and says, "Woman though art loosed from thine infirmity." Woman you are released, set free, no longer detained by what cripples you; you are free from your weakness.

Jesus lifts her from shame to a place of honor. Jesus is the only one who can set the captive free. Jesus spoke the word, laid his hands on the woman, and she was healed. A divine reversal took place. The woman was immediately made straight and she began to glorify God.

What is the appropriate action to take when you come in contact with God's grace?

Proof of the woman's restoration is immediate. She is immediately able to stand straight and glorify God, which is the only appropriate response to God's redemptive power. This was a synagogue service the people never forgot. It was a day when a woman received her liberation.

But here is the paradox: her *liberation* led to *indignation*. The text says the leader of the synagogue was indignant because Jesus healed on the Sabbath. Instead of rejoicing and glorifying God as they witnessed God's manifestation right before their eyes, the ruler of the synagogue became very angry (see Luke 8:41). You would think the leader of the faith community would celebrate with the woman! Rather, the ruler of the synagogue challenged Jesus.

The ruler of the synagogue said, "There are six days on which it is necessary to work; so come on those days to be healed, and not on the Sabbath day." Notice it was okay to attend worship in the synagogue but do not attend with the hope of being healed.

Contemporary readers cannot understand why the synagogue leaders would express such indignation with this woman's liberation. Why wouldn't they celebrate this woman's deliverance! Eighteen years is a long time. It's a long time to be sick. It's a long time to be unemployed. It's a long time to be isolated. Eighteen years is a long time! And the synagogue ruler said, "We don't heal on the Sabbath." This reaction reminds me of the meetings we have, in the name of God, for the sake of God, but we don't necessarily want a real movement in spite of God.

Don't break the rules. Sometimes we allow our pursuit of religious practices to outweigh our responsibility to be compassionate. The synagogue leader responds with indignation because the Sabbath was not the appropriate day on which to heal. Although what the synagogue ruler said was important, *why* he said it is even more important to the story.

For you see, his indignation was a matter of interpretation. The attitude of the synagogue leader was informed by his *interpretation* of the law—that one should deliberately avoid treating nonfatal wounds and injuries on the Sabbath.

In other words, it was permissible to treat what was considered a *critical* condition but not a *chronic* one—meaning it was permissible to treat her condition had it involved immediate danger or death.

The ruler's attitude was that this woman's condition was *chronic* and not critical. Her situation did not have the urgency of something like childbirth, a heart attack, or a stroke. It was much closer to the case of the broken limb or dislocated arm. So, because the woman had a chronic condition, in the leader's mind, one more day would not have made a difference. It would have been better to wait another day rather than violate the Sabbath.

Isn't it funny how there is always somebody who always wants to say that one more day won't kill you? Although the leader of the synagogue's indignation is due to his concern for the proper observance of the Sabbath rather than celebration of the woman's release from her condition, Jesus responds to his indignation with *a word of vindication*.

Jesus says, "You hypocrites, doesn't each of you untie or loose his ox or donkey from the stall and lead it out to give it water? Then should not this woman, a daughter of Abraham whom Satan has kept bound for eighteen long years, be set free on the Sabbath day from what bound her." In other words, Jesus is saying, "She ain't got to wait another day!"

You may have a chronic condition. Critical means it's urgent. Chronic implies that something has been going on for a long time. You've been depressed a long time. You have been frustrated a long time. You have been tired a long time. You have been disillusioned a long time. You have been waiting a long time. You have been praying a long time. If you do not have a chronic condition, you may find yourself ministering to someone whose liberation has been suppressed. In other words, you have been in a position of powerlessness, helplessness, defeat, and impotence for so long that it has become normative for you.

Some of us have been in situations and conditions for so long that we have accepted it as a way of life. But thank God, on that day in the synagogue, Jesus made an urgent utterance because he understood the fierce urgency of now. Some things just can't wait another eighteen years. The blood of Trayvon Martin demanded that we not wait another eighteen days to decry his death. The release of Anthony Graves from prison after being on death row for eighteen years demanded that he not wait another day in jail. People who have been wrongfully imprisoned don't have the luxury of waiting another day. People who can't feed their families can't wait another day. Men, women, and children who are in need of health care can't wait another day. There are seniors who are on Medicaid who can't wait another day. And you may not be able to wait another eighteen years, eighteen months, eighteen weeks, eighteen hours, eighteen minutes, or even eighteen seconds. You need a breakthrough right now!

There will always be somebody who will say, "Not yet." When blacks were in slavery, the white supremacists said, "Not yet." When blacks were freed from slavery, Jim Crow said, "Not yet." When blacks fought for the right to vote, somebody said, "Not yet." When a black man from the Southside of Chicago believed he could be president of the United States, somebody said, "Not yet." When woman felt a call to preach, there were some who said and still say, "Not yet." When Christ Missionary Baptist Church in Memphis, Tennessee, pondered electing a female as their pastor, somebody said, "Not yet." There will always be someone who will say, "Not yet."

But thank God, Jesus declares that healing for this woman is "mission critical." It was critical enough to break the rules, critical enough to set her free on the Sabbath, and critical enough to release her from her infirmity. There is something grossly hypocritical about treating animals better than people. There's something grossly hypocritical about locking up Michael Vick for illegal dog fighting but allowing criminals to never be charged with murder. There's something grossly hypocritical when people can get in an uproar about abortion but think nothing of starving children after they are born and the elderly when they reach old age.

There's something grossly hypocritical about trying to make decisions about a woman's reproductive choices. There's something grossly hypocritical when we can bomb abortion clinics in the name of God but have regard for the sanctity of life.

Jesus says *anytime* is the right time to exercise the ministry to release the bondage of Satan. *Anytime* is the right time for a demonstration of God's compassion. *Anytime* is the right time to access the power of God. *Anytime* is the right time to access God's presence.

Tell somebody about the fierce urgency of now! The thief comes to kill, steal, and destroy, but Jesus says, I have come that you may have life and have it more abundantly—not next week, not next month, not next year, but right now!!

This is the message to preach and proclaim! Oppression doesn't have to have the last word! Some of us will come in contact with people who are bent out of shape from trying to meet others' expectations. They are bent over from suffering, bent over from sin, bent over from sorrow, bent over by insecurity, bent over by shame, bent over because of marginalization, bent over by victimization, bent over by isolation, bent over from poverty, and bent over from a broken justice system.

There are some folks who don't have another eighteen years, eighteen months, eighteen days, eighteen minutes, or eighteen seconds. But we can announce that God has and is already acting on our behalf. Just as Jesus met that woman in the synagogue, I am so glad that Jesus will meet us right where we are. Jesus will meet you where you are. Jesus will speak to you, pronounce you restored, touch you, defend you against your opponents, and welcome you to be a part of the family of God.

Whatever the problem, whatever the challenge, whatever the situation, Jesus offers a deliverance that is designed to free us to relate to him in a way that enables us to shed the limitations Satan sometimes chains us with.

There is always somebody who wants to say it can wait. Your deliverance can wait. Your freedom can wait. Your ministry can wait. Your liberation can wait. Jesus says, you don't have to wait another day.

Establishing a relationship with God and the access to the power of God's presence in God's Spirit empowers us with resources to renew our lives. Any time is appropriate for such a move towards restoration. It is what Jesus' ministry—and the church's ministry—is all about.

Jesus gave his life for our restoration. Your full restoration may not be all at once like the woman's in this story. It may have to wait until we meet our God face to face. But this woman's healing is our clue that the reign of God's wholeness has begun.

CHAPTER 21

I'M IN A NEW PLACE

Neichelle R. Guidry Jones

Read: Luke 1:39–56

Ilove the women of the Bible. I love that the women of the Bible are depicted as *humans* with complex stories.

There were women who were rejected and women who ruled from palm trees, women with great names such as *Vashti, Esther*— and women with no names, such as *Jephthah's daughter*, the *Shulamite woman*, and the *woman with the issue of blood*. Now, the *only* thing I love more than the women of the Bible is the *work* that God does in the lives of the women of the Bible.

I love wombs that were written off as empty, suddenly being filled with human embryos. I love God showing up at rivers and creeks to encounter disinherited women and say, "I see you." I *love* healing shooting into a woman's body from an article of clothing that was attached to the body of Christ. I love the dispensation of grace that occurred when a woman bowed down and anointed Jesus' feet with her hair, her tears, and her oil. And I love when God does something in a woman's life and suddenly she *breaks out* in song! What I see when women break out into song in the scriptures is that they have been shifted into a new place—moved from one place to another.

Songs signify new places, and so it was in the case of Miriam's song in Exodus 15:20.

And there is a song here in Luke 1 where we are allowed into the backstory of the birth of Jesus Christ. In this backstory, we learn that a *whole* lot went on before Jesus was born, and a *whole* bunch of women had a *whole* lot to do with it. I believe there are a few women who know what it feels like to be in the backstory. You're used to your quiet place in the background where no one knows who you are. You know what it feels like to be behind the veil, cranking the well so the water will flow or at the helm, turning the wheel so the ship can stay on course. But it always seems as if your part is the part skipped when the story is told. Why? Because you're in the backstory.

There's another woman in the Bible who stands in community with those of us who are in the backstories of our congregations, organizations, workplaces, and even our families. However, this woman's story tells us that in the course of *one* divine conversation or with *one* word, God can move us out of the backstory and into the script. Very quickly, God can move us into a *new place*. This woman's name is Mary. You can say that in the course of twelve short verses, Mary was divinely shifted from an old place to a new place.

Do you know what it feels like to be moved from one place to another place? For good or for bad? Whether you wanted to be moved or not? When it seems as if God has stepped into your familiar, gotten right behind you, and bumped you out of it? When it feels like God took God's mighty, powerful, providing, and protecting hand, *snatched* you, and seemingly *threw* you into a new place with no power, no provision, no protection? Or maybe you've felt thrown into a place of GREATER power, GREATER provision, and GREATER protection, but you had no idea what to do with all of it. Maybe it seems as if God has approached you, real coolly, on the sly, and almost whispered, "Sis, it's time to move. Let's go."

Well, what does it mean to get moved? Beyond the obvious fact that we can't stay in the same place forever, *why* does God move us? And most importantly, what are the assurances that *hold* us in our new places? Let's look to Luke.

The first thing we see is that forward movement is a mark of favor. "Greetings," said Gabriel, "you who are highly favored!" Now, favor has a great reputation in the church. "Favor ain't fair!" we say! We proclaim with great excitement that *favor* opens doors, increases net worth, and puts us before mighty and powerful men and women. In this text, however, I see a very different theology of favor. Notice the order of things here: the greeting and affirmation of favor *and then* the shift. Sometimes God has to remind you that you are loved, favored, and covered right before your assurance in these things comes under fire. The text says Mary was very "perplexed" at this greeting. Mary had the right to be. God was up to something. God wanted something from Mary. It's almost as if God was saying to her: *I know you're young and you had a nice, run-of-the-mill plan for your life, but I am requiring more of you. Mary, I need you to know I have gifted you and I have prepared you. I've brought you through all you've come through and I can use you in ways I can't use anybody else and I need you right now. So now I'm about to move you. You're about to be moved into a new place because I've been watching you. And I see something in you—something that I placed in you a long time ago—that will bring me glory.*

Let me suggest a new favor theology. Perhaps God will disrupt your comfort because God favors you. Perhaps God will frustrate your plans because God favors you. Perhaps the point of favor is not for you to accumulate more, but for you to come to see in yourself what God sees in you! Shift you until you proclaim, "I never knew I had this kind of strength, or this kind of resilience. I never knew I had the skill of adjusting until God moved me. Wow! All of this is in *me*? I *am* favored!" Good news! Right before God dropped the bomb.

The second thing we see in this text is that Mary raised a *question*: "How will this be since I am a virgin?" Perplexed, Mary sought some wisdom from God: "God, there are some experiences I have not had. Some experiences which are usually required for this kind of thing. How are you going to move me into a new place when I haven't had the experience that is required for me to do the thing I have to do in the new place?" And it was a good question because we often worry about *qualification*. Do we have the background, experience, or education to do well in a new place? New places can also be daunting due to questions regarding our *preparation*. Have you ever asked the question, *"Am I really ready for this?"* Well, my sister, the text is telling us we may or may not have the qualification or preparation, but when God shifts us into a new place, we need more than these anyway.

"How will this be," Mary asked. "Baby," Gabriel responded. "The *Holy Spirit* will come upon you and the *power of the Most High* will overcome you." In other words, this wasn't about Mary and what she could or couldn't do on her own.

When God shifts you into new places, you need a *power* that is greater than your own. There will be new experiences—let the Spirit guide you. New people—let the Spirit show you who is for you and who is against you. New problems and predicaments—let the Spirit give you wisdom. It will be unfamiliar—let the Spirit show you around. It will be uncomfortable—let the Spirit hold you and comfort you.

Finally, the text says, "Then the angel departed from her." Have you ever been there: *Seriously, God? You gonna tell me something like that and then just . . . bounce? You gonna get my YES and then go?*

Sometimes our new places can be isolating. We have to find new communities, new girlfriends. Here in the text, when Mary felt isolated and abandoned, she had to get moving. And not just moving around anxiously. She went to Elizabeth. She went to someone who was on the same path and who had been on the path a little longer than she. She went somewhere where she knew she could hear a word of encouragement and receive some comfort. When she got to Elizabeth's house, Elizabeth was filled with the Holy Spirit upon hearing Mary's greeting, upon encountering Mary in her new place.

Here, there are two lessons. First, sometimes, you need to push back against loneliness and isolation. You need to go in search of some friendship. Second, you need to go and be with somebody who sees, feels, and discerns your gifts and gets *excited* for what God is about to do through you. Sometimes you need to hear somebody say, "God is doing great things in your life!" You need to be around somebody who will suspend jealousy and judgment and hateration to *celebrate* you in your new place. You need somebody whose gifts and anointing cause her to *jump around* when you are close by. Girl, you are in a new place and you will need someone to cheer you on, to cover you in prayer, and hold your arms up. You need someone to BREAK OUT IN SONG WITH YOU!

I wonder if there are any sisters who need a girlfriend with whom they can sing a song. Do you need a girlfriend to support you in your new place? Do you need a cheerleader to cheer you on? Well, here you go! You are surrounded by a sisterhood who is ready to sing a song of praise for all that God is doing in your life!

As a matter of fact, I'm in need of a song myself. God is doing some things in my life, and I'm on the market for a few girlfriends who can praise God with me. I'm looking for some women who can seek God's face with me, fast, and pray with me, and give God a premature praise with me! I'm seeking some sistahs who are willing to break out in song *together.* I believe once we all begin to sing a song of praise together, our new places won't be as scary. We won't be as timid because *we have* each other and *we have* the power of the Spirit. And because that's mighty good reason to sing, I believe "*I will bless the Lord at all times! God's praise will continually be in my mouth. My soul shall make her boast in the Lord. The humble shall hear thereof and be glad. Oh, magnify the Lord with me, my sisters, let us exalt God's name together.*"

In the name of God who favors us enough to let us go through some stuff, who loves us enough to give us the Spirit, who calls us out of isolation into song, and the God who calls us into a new place.

CHAPTER 22

YOU FEED THEM

Ella Pearson Mitchell

Read: Luke 9:13 KJV, TLB, NIV, and NSV

It has been a remarkable four days for me, supposedly retired, and long since of the retirement vintage. You see, I continue to stand in need of Sabbath rest myself, and God's alternating cycles of labor and rest are as important for me as anybody. So I thank God for this Sabbath rest, and for all of you.

I have been asked to take you with me to a desert place near Bethsaida, and to help us all to enter into the disciples' experience there, as recorded in the lesson from Luke 9:10–17. The disciples have just come in from a demanding tour of duty as "practice preachers," so to speak. They happily report to Jesus all they have accomplished in the hard places to which they have been sent, and under the rigorous rules Jesus has laid down. They are typically required to carry no money or extra clothing, and they are to share the living conditions of the people among whom they seek to serve. They are exhausted—dead tired both in body and in spirit. Nevertheless, they are elated that they have scored extremely well with the people.

Jesus senses their exhaustion and takes them some distance to an uninhibited and uncultivated spot near Bethsaida—a place well fitted for use as a kind of retreat center. The disciples relish these times with Jesus, and are delighted to get away for a while. Just how long that while turns out to be we don't really know, but it isn't very long in any case.

We do know that the disciples have been so effective that the crowd wants more. Perhaps one person happens to have seen the direction in which they were headed when they left town, and slowly but surely the word spreads. It takes only a day or two for the word to reach most of the town or village, and for the people to proceed en masse to move on to the disciples' once quiet place of retreat.

Jesus feels compelled to turn his attention to teaching and healing this crowd, estimated by some to be in the thousands. This huge crowd is deeply engrossed in what Jesus is saying and doing. They listen so eagerly and intently that the whole day slips by without a count of how many hours have passed. The disciples suddenly realize that it's getting late. They are so deeply concerned about what's going on around them that they get up the nerve to interrupt Jesus as he is teaching on his favorite subject, the kingdom of God. They press on him their suggestion that he ought to send these folks away, before it gets too dark, and in time for them to get something for their evening meal. The disciples are worried 'cause they themselves haven't had a bite to eat all day.

Jesus' response to their apparently sound suggestion is that they seat this huge crowd in groups of fifty and, *would you believe?* Proceed to feed the crowd themselves! The disciples, in utter amazement, reply that the only food they've seen is some kid's bag lunch, and that has only five barley buns and a couple of small fish. In their minds they are complaining, something like I once heard a Louisiana brother put it graphically: "We need a couple of supermarkets for this bunch, and we haven't even got a mom-and-pop corner grocery nearby."

Incredulous as they are, the disciples decide, reluctantly, to obey their Lord. They organize the crowd and ask this lad for his lunch. Jesus says the blessing over it and breaks it up like Communion. He gives the broken fragments to the disciples to distribute. Wow! To their absolute amazement, the crowd is fully fed. How this happens the Gospel writer forgets to give us the details about. He is kind enough to tell us, for sure, that they have to look around for a dozen baskets so they can collect the leftovers. Not much of an overage for so large a crowd, but the point is that there was plenty!

The awesome amount they actually eat is what has puzzled most people ever since the invention of the printing press, if not much earlier. It has troubled me a little since I was a child. But I really pondered it in full color again recently, when our granddaughter, Lt. Stephanie Mitchell-Smith, proudly escorted us aboard the USS

Enterprise. They had stacks and stacks of food being loaded on the deck, and even with all that, I still wondered how on earth or sea they could feed a crew that numbered four to six thousand, and three meals per day! When they were way out there in the middle of the ocean, it had to be a monster of an assignment. The task was hard enough, just feeding that many when they were tied to the dock. Then I thought, "Jesus had no forklifts and trucks, no squads of crewmen, and the twelve disciples had only their bare hands. How? How? How?" This thing in my mind was getting out of control. I decided to forget all these questions about the historicity, statistics, and mechanics of the feeding of the five thousand before I got a severe headache. I settled for a devout and dedicated scholar's idea that "we can with good reason think in terms of Jesus feeding a large number of people with an impossibly small quantity of food" (John Nolland, *Word Biblical Commentary*, vol. 35A, 445).

Meanwhile, in the midst of this impressive but perplexing account, the original author is clearly offering us a major lesson. In Luke's world, eating with people is highly significant. Meals are sacraments full of meaning, Jesus' charge to the disciples is "You feed them," and the way he broke the bread is significant. It involves far more than the simple response required for physical hunger. It is this "more than" concerning which I feel called to address.

As we depart this place, Jesus' charge to feed the crowd following their retreat echoes in our souls. We, too, are compelled by the realities of our time to wonder how on earth we are to feed such a host, and in the midst of so much obvious oppression, exploitation, confusion, and demonic destruction. My husband and I teach against this sort of catalogue of catastrophes, but I must share with you some of the less evident but terror-striking facts that lie alongside the obvious—dope, divorce, delinquency, deadly violence, and adolescent parenthood. We are more and more hard put to find high-caliber candidates for political office, with a resulting decrease in confidence in government. Fourteen major cities are without services of school superintendents because of disarray in school boards as they confront the failures of the schools. And even when they get a good superintendent, they run her or him away in less than three years on the average. With our public schools in shambles and dangerously tempted to abdicate to profit-seeking private enterprise, we are bereft of hope at the precise point where our future depends most on it. I need to cease this horror story, but I have to give closing mention to one fact concerning the state of religion in America: without major changes in prevalent trends, congregations and denominations as we know them can be predicted to be dead and gone in another fifty to seventy-five years.

Our hearts cry out, "and, Lord, you want us to feed them? Look how many there are and how great is their hunger! Surely you don't expect us to feed so many, when they need so many, when they need so much! Here and there a child rises up in awesome achievement, and we see a glimmer of hope notwithstanding—only to have some other kid shoot up his entire school. Do you realize what you are sending us back to, with only a few days' rest?"

The calm, firm reply comes back, "Yes, you feed them." My beloved, it's not like God doesn't hear us, or that God hears and ignores our profound sense of inadequacy. O, yes, God does hear, and does understand our deep concerns. And to cap it all, that firmness of response has about it an aura of compassion. Yet, our Lord does not yield to our pitiful pleas. Rather, the look in those eyes seems almost to be saying, "Surely you don't think I have not seen what you will face. Did I not weep over Jerusalem?"

We get the point, and our love for our Lord gets the upper hand over our worldly prudence. Almost in a daze, we walk up obediently and gather the fragments of the meal, which we are called to distribute. As we turn to face a needy world, we still wonder in retrospect, "What were the sources of supply that Luke failed to mention?" And we'd give much to know also, "What went through the disciples' minds as they received so little in their hands? The sea of expectant faces to which we return overwhelms our hesitancy, and we move to give them what we have, little as it may seem.

Is that same instant the hosts of heaven swing into awesome action. Innumerable resources pour forth from the pantries of the Spirit. As we pass among the numberless needy, there seems to course through our veins a power greater than we have ever known. And our hands are suddenly filled with that which feeds the souls of them that look to us—those who sought us—those who drew us away from our Sabbath rest.

As our Master was recognized in the breaking of bread at the home in Emmaus, so also will our Lord be met in the serving of the various breads of living, which come from the vast and plentiful pantry of the Spirit. The more we confront the needs of humankind, the more we are supplied from that pantry. Whether we are in places of easy access or places comparable to the high seas, the bread will reach us on time, in the right place, and not a meal will be missed, no matter how many there are to feed . . . to be fed.

It may sound too poetic for the real world, but if you summon a fellow named Peter, he will tell you how it happened for him. He will tell you that the pantry of the Spirit is not just a mystical vision, or worse, a wishful figment of a desperate imagination. I tell you, this limitless pantry happened, and it still happens, and it will continue to.

Peter, you will remember, was the fellow who denied the Lord three times. Yet he was used by the Lord to exemplify the rock-like faith on which the church of Jesus Christ was to be built. This rough, vociferous, unlettered fisherman was confronted at Pentecost with thousands of curiosity seekers. Apart from brief stints of practice preaching when the disciples were sent out, he had no real training. At best his preparation was far from complete. Under such circumstances how did he dare try to live up to those thrice-repeated commands, feed my lambs, feed my sheep; feed my sheep? (John 21:15–17, parphrased). How could he live up to that passionate promise he made?

Those thousands were standing there waiting! He had prayed in the upper room, and he prayed some more, still painfully aware of his inadequate mind and spirit. Then he opened his mouth in faithful obedience, to see what God would manage to do with the best he had to offer.

Guess what?! God actually fed them! God fed them well!

In what must have been a huge surprise to Peter, not only did they listen, not only did they receive intently, but thousands were converted. Nothing Peter had ever done before or would do even afterwards ever matched the response of that crowd that day. Peter did the best he could to obey God's "You feed them," and God took over from there, reaching into the unlimited supplies, the constantly replenished pantry of the Spirit,

Peter's experience is neither unique nor limited in time. May I tell you of my experience of some forty years ago?

It was in the San Jose area in northern Californina. Hundreds of our people had moved there, because the Ford assembly plant had moved from Richmond to Milpitas. Reverend (let's call him Jones) had decided to start a church there, to meet the needs of the folks moving in. They were having to assemble in an auto repair garage until they could locate a better place to worship. Reverend Jones had invited me to speak for Women's Day. Notice I didn't say "preach," and this was evidenced by the fact that I was allowed to speak from the floor, not the pulpit. The place was crowded with 150 or more people, some of them obviously not very happy to even see a woman as the speaker that morning,

To add to the discomfort of crowding in, it should be noted that the seats were of the improvised variety. Standing there on the floor and looking into their not-always-welcoming eyes, I hardly knew what to say. Well, I prayed a little prayer, and the Lord helped me get myself together, and then I just preached the Word the very best I could. It wasn't too terribly long before I began to see and hear some evidence that these saints were being fed. The response grew more and more outspoken, and I gained more and more courage. The holy ecstasy I began to sense in myself seemed to embrace not only the few old veteran Christians; it was claiming some manifestly young adults. The shouting spread among young and old.

Eleven persons came eagerly seeking to unite with the church. A giant of a thirty-five-year-old man shouted as I had never seen any male shout before, and that whole garage was set aflame with spiritual fire. I had to know that I wasn't responsible for this marvelously moving experience. I just bowed my head and sobbed for holy joy. The pantry of the Spirit had supplied whatever was needed, and above and beyond my feeble effort in that garage. That place that had been less than hospitable to me at first was now bursting with the fruits of the Spirit.

It is now that I can begin to sense how Peter must have felt that day the church was first launched in Jerusalem. And I know far better than I did what Jesus meant when he said so simply, "You feed them." It wasn't with the clear assurance that "When I tell you to feed them, it's because I have already provided in the pantry of the Spirit everything you will ever need for the task." Jesus was saying, "Whatever your limitation, I declare unto you, 'You can feed them.' However uncomfortable the setting, and no matter how much you feel you need more rest, you can feed them. No matter how much you would welcome more experience before your trial by fire, you can feed them. Even though I will keep on teaching you and helping you to grow, you have to start where you are, and even there you can feed them. So long as you prepare to give your very best and to give all you have, with the help from the Spirit-filled pantry, you can feed them."

I know this for sure when I read sermons that I wrote and God used forty, thirty, even twenty years ago. I know that when our resources have been exhausted, that which is needed will be supplied from the limitless pantry of the Spirit, and you and I will be messengers for the feeding of all God's children. Yea, each and every time there will be some left over.

And so, O Lord, we leave this place praying only that following this Sabbath, we may be used to feed your people from baskets that overflow. Amen.

CONTRIBUTORS

Rev. Felicia Sophronia Barwell is the associate minister and youth minister at Faith Community Baptist Church. She received her masters of divinity degree (MDiv) from the Samuel Dewitt Proctor School of Theology at Virginia Union University in 2010 and a bachelor of science (BS) degree from St. Augustine College in Raleigh, North Carolina. She served in the United States Army and the Army Reserve for twenty-eight years. Rev. Barwell achieved the rank of lieutenant colonel and served a year in Iraq in 2005–2006. For this service, she was awarded the Bronze Star, the Global War on Terrorism Medal, the Iraq Campaign Medal, and several Joint medals.

Rev. Dr. Gwendolyn E. Boyd was the twenty-second national president of Delta Sigma Theta Sorority, Inc., the nation's largest African American public service sorority. She earned a bachelor's degree in mathematics from Alabama State University and a master's degree in mechanical engineering from Yale University, where she was the only woman and the only African American among her program's twenty-five students. She joined the Johns Hopkins Applied Physics Lab in 1980 and today is executive assistant to the chief of staff. Rev. Boyd serves on the ministerial staff at Ebenezer African Methodist Episcopal (AME) Church in Fort Washington, Maryland. Among her numerous honors, she was appointed by President Obama to serve as a member of the Board of Trustees, Barry Goldwater Scholarship and Excellence in Education Foundation.

Rev. Dr. Marie Murphy Phillips Braxton is the assistant pastor at the Metropolitan AME Church in Washington, DC. She has done graduate studies at the St. Mary's Theological Seminary, Norfolk State University, and Western Maryland College. She holds a master of divinity degree from the Samuel DeWitt Proctor School of Theology at Virginia Union University and a doctor of ministry degree from the United Theological Seminary, Dayton, Ohio. In addition, Rev. Braxton is employed as a crisis counselor for the Prince George's County Public Schools.

Rev. Dr. Jo Ann Browning graduated from Boston University in 1976 with a bachelor of science (BS) degree in communications. She received a master of divinity (MDiv) degree in 1986 and a doctorate of ministry (DMin) from Howard University School of Divinity in 1991. A recognized trailblazer and community leader, Dr. Browning has received numerous awards and accolades. In 2006, she received an honorary doctor of divinity degree from AME University in Monrovia, Liberia. In 2007, she was honored to preach Spelman College's baccalaureate ceremony, where she also served on the Spelman Colleges Sistah's Chapel Wisdom Center Executive Board.

Rev. Elizabeth Mitchell Clement is the associate director for Leadership Gifts Financial Development for the United Church of Christ. She is a graduate of Talladega College and received an MDiv (cum laude) from the Candler School of Theology at Emory University. Rev. Clement holds a professional certification in translation and interpreting (French and English) from Georgia State University. From 2002 to 2004, Rev. Clement served as Dean of Spiritual and Ethical Life at Deerfield Academy in Massachusetts, where she also taught ethics and an introduction to the Bible.

Rev. Dr. Judy D. Cummings was called as the first woman to pastor the historic New Covenant Christian Church (Disciples of Christ) in its 152 years of existence. Under her visionary leadership, New Covenant has grown spiritually and numerically. Rev. Cummings holds degrees from Tennessee State University School of Nursing and the University of St. Francis, MDiv from the Southern Baptist Theological Seminary, and DMin in preaching and church leadership from Asbury Theological Seminary.

Minister Carla J. Debnam is the associate minister of Morning Star Baptist Church, Catonsville, Maryland. She has a master of science degree in pastoral counseling from Loyola University Maryland and is currently pursuing a doctor of ministry degree (DMin) in transformational leadership from the Ashland Theological Seminary in Ashland, Ohio. She is a national certified counselor (NCC) and licensed clinical professional counselor (LCPC). Minister Debnam is currently the executive director of the Renaissance Center in Woodlawn, Maryland, a Christian counseling center that has been in existence since July 2001 and is an outreach ministry of Morning Star Baptist Church in Catonsville, Maryland.

Rev. Dr. Frances "Toni" Murphy Draper is the visionary and founding pastor of the Freedom Temple African Methodist Episcopal Zion Church in Brooklyn, Maryland (formerly known as John Wesley AME Zion Church). Dr. Draper attended Morgan State University, earning a bachelor of arts degree in Spanish education, and Johns Hopkins University, earning a master of education degree. Dr. Draper also earned a master of business administration (MBA) degree from the University of Maryland and picked up graduate credits at St. Mary's Seminary before receiving a master of science degree in pastoral counseling from Loyola College in Baltimore. Rev. Draper received her DMin from United Seminary in Dayton, Ohio. Since 1995, she has been a gubernatorial appointee to the Morgan State University Board of Regents, where she serves as board secretary.

Rev. Sekinah Hamlin is an ordained minister of the gospel of Jesus Christ in the Christian Church (Disciples of Christ) tradition. She earned a bahelor of arts degree from Bennett College for Women and an master of arts from Howard University, both in political science. Rev. Hamlin also earned an MDiv from Duke University Divinity School, and she is a Cornell University Certified Diversity Professional.

Rev. Dr. Monica Hardy-McCray is the senior pastor of the Tabernacle International Deliverance Ministry. She received her bachelor of science degree in health information management from Florida A&M University, master of arts degree in management and human resource development from Webster University, doctor of education degree from Nova Southeastern University, and doctor of ministry (DMin) degree from Refreshing Faith Bible College.

Rev. Corliss D. Heath obtained a bachelor of science degree in mathematics from Clark Atlanta University in 1993. In 1998 she received a master of public health degree and in 2004 received a master of divinity degree, both from Emory University. Currently she is a doctoral candidate at the University of South Florida (Tampa), specializing in biocultural medical anthropology. Rev. Corliss Heath is an itinerant elder in the African Methodist Episcopal Church and the past health director for the Sixth Episcopal District

Rev. Dr. Jessica Kendell Ingram currently serves as the Episcopal supervisor for the Tenth Episcopal District of the African Methodist Episcopal Church. This district encompasses the state of Texas. Dr. Ingram earned a BA in special education from the University of Missouri, an MA in guidance and counseling from St. Louis University, a master of religious education degree from Garrett Evangelical Theological Seminary, and a DMin in spirituality from United Theological Seminary. Dr. Ingram was featured in *Ebony* magazine as one of the Fifteen Top African American Female Preachers in the United States. *The African American Pulpit* named her one of the 20 Great African American Revivalists of the Century.

Rev. Neichelle R. Guidry Jones currently serves as the associate pastor to young adults at Trinity United Church of Christ on the south side of Chicago. She is a graduate of Clark Atlanta University (2007, BA, religion and mass media arts) and Yale Divinity School (2010, MDiv). As a current Fund for Theological Education doctoral fellow, Neichelle is a current PhD student in liturgical studies at Garrett-Evangelical Theological Seminary in Evanston, Illinois.

Rev. Carolyn Ann Knight received her early education in the public school system in Denver and a bachelor of arts degree from Bishop College in Dallas, Texas, with a major concentration in English, philosophy, and religion. Her theological training began at Colgate Rochester Divinity School in Rochester, New York; she later transferred to Union Theological Seminary in New York City to study under her mentor, Dr. Cornel West. She received the doctor of ministry degree from United Theological Seminary in Dayton, Ohio. She is the founder and president of "CAN DO!" Ministries, a progressive, preventive youth advocacy ministry that is dedicated to the cultural, social, intellectual, and spiritual well-being of youth and young adults.

Minister Cheryl A. Lindsay attended the University of Pennsylvania and earned a bachelor of science degree in economics with a concentration in marketing. She is a 2012 honors graduate from Ashland Theological Seminary, where she received a master of divinity degree with a concentration in evangelism and church renewal. In 2008, she accepted the call to pastoral ministry and has been an active member of the ministerium of Mt. Zion Congregational Church, United Church of Christ.

Rev. Angelique Mason is the pastor of the historic Allen African Methodist Episcopal Church in Hillsboro, Maryland. In 1995, she was ordained an itinerant elder in the African American Episcopal Church. She began her ministry at the Oak Street AME Church under the pastorate and leadership of her spiritual mother, Bishop Vashti Murphy McKenzie. Rev. Mason earned a bachelor of science degree in business administration from Morgan State University and an MDiv from Howard University School of Divinity.

Rev. Sheila R. McKeithen defied the odds in 1986 when the doctors assured her that she had less than six days to live. More than twenty-five years later, she has achieved her dream of becoming an attorney at law, having served as a former local bar association president and former board member for Legal Aid of Broward County and the Florida Law Related Association. At the height of her legal career, when she served as assistant attorney general (Florida), she was ordained and assigned to minister in Jamaica for six months. Today that assignment continues in her role as senior minister of the Universal Centre of Truth for Better Living in Kingston, Jamaica.

Bishop Vashti Murphy McKenzie serves as the 117th elected and consecrated bishop of the African Methodist Episcopal Church. Her historic election in the year 2000 represents the first time in the 213-year history of the AME Church that a woman obtained the level of Episcopal office. Currently, she is the presiding prelate of the Tenth Episcopal District, which includes the state of Texas. McKenzie holds an MDiv from Howard University School of Divinity and a DMin from United Theological Seminary in Dayton, Ohio. Bishop McKenzie was appointed to serve on the Advisory Council of the White House Faith-Based and Neighborhood Partnerships by President Barack Obama in 2009. She is vice-chair of the Board of Trustees of Paul Quinn College in Dallas, Texas, and is also a member of the Board of Trustees of the International Theological Center in Atlanta, Georgia. Bishop McKenzie is a best-selling author of The Pilgrim Press with her books *Not without a Struggle: Leadership Development for African American Women in Ministry, Revised and Updated*; *Strength in the Struggle: Leadership for Women in Ministry*; and *Swapping Housewives: Rachel and Jacob and Leah*.

Rev. Dr. Ella Pearson Mitchell was a pioneer in African American preaching and religious education. Her reputation as a promoter and encourager of women in ministry earned her the title "Dean of African American women preachers." Dr. Mitchell broke down many barriers, achieving a number of "firsts" for women in ministry. She was the first female dean of Sisters Chapel, Spelman College, Atlanta, Georgia, and the first woman to preach at Hampton Ministerial Conference, Hampton, Virginia. A graduate of Columbia University Teachers College and United Theological Seminary in New York City, she earned a doctor of ministry degree from Claremont School of Theology in Claremont, CA. Dr. Mitchell died on November 19, 2008, at the age of ninety-one.

Rev. Vashti-Jasmine McKenzie Saint-Jean is the community supervision officer at the Court Services and Offender Supervision Agency for the District of Columbia. She holds an MDiv in youth ministry and church administration from Garrett Evangelical Theological Seminary, a certificate in youth and theology, youth ministry from Princeton Theological Seminary, and a BA in administration of justice from Howard University.

Rev. Dr. Carolyn D. Showell is an ordained minister in the Pentecostal Assemblies of the World, Inc. Committed to being a lifelong student, Rev. Showell was awarded a BA degree from Goucher College, and an MDiv degree from Union Theological Seminary of New York, with a concentration in psychology and theology. She received her PhD in counseling psychology from the Carolina University of Theology. She is a certified licensed therapist and pastoral counselor. Additionally, she has completed all course requirements for a second doctoral program in Jewish and biblical studies at the Baltimore Hebrew University and the Advanced Studies Program in Psychology at Loyola University. Dr. Showell is a gifted and anointed speaker who serves as a church transformation consultant to many of our country's most dynamic ministries, and she is the recipient of numerous awards, honors, and scholarships.

Rev. Dr. Gina Stewart is senior pastor at Christ Missionary Baptist Church. She earned a bachelor of business administration (BBA) in marketing from the University of Memphis and a master of education degree in administration and supervision from Trevecca Nazarene College in Nashville, Tennessee. Rev. Stewart received an MDiv from Memphis Theological Seminary and attended the Harvard Divinity School Summer Leadership Institute for Church Based Community and Economic Development. She received a DMin from Interdenominational Theological Center (ITC). Rev. Stewart has served as a team leader for the Pastoral Excellence Program for Lott Carey International, a development and advocacy organization. She serves as an adjunct professor for Memphis Theological Seminary and a visiting professor of practical theology for the Samuel D. Proctor School of Theology at Virginia Union University.